THE HIGHWAY IS FOR GAMBLERS

A POLITICAL MEMOIR

Tom O'Lincoln
with Janey Stone

INTERVENTIONS
MELBOURNE

© Tom O'Lincoln 2017

Published in 2017 by Interventions

Interventions is a not-for-profit, independent left wing book publisher. For further information:
    www.interventions.org.au
    admin@interventions.org.au
    Trades Hall Suite 68
    54 Victoria Street
    Carlton VIC 3053

Cover and layout design by Viktoria Ivanova
Printed and bound in Australia by ImpactDigital

Cover images: Tom O'Lincoln and Janey Stone at a demonstration outside Australia House in London, July 1975; SWAG members at a demonstration (Tess Lee Ack holding 'strike now' placard; Tom with brother Terry and mother Evelyn; Tom
Back cover image: Tom in 1973

National Library of Australia Cataloguing-in-Publication entry

Creator: O'Lincoln, Tom, author

Title: The highway is for gamblers: a political memoir / Tom O'Lincoln, with Janey Stone

    ISBN: 9780994537829 (paperback)

Notes: Includes bibliographical references

Subjects: O'Lincoln, Tom
O'Lincoln, Tom--Political activity
Socialists--Biography
Political activists--Biography
Philosophy, Marxist

Other Creators/Contributors:
Stone, Janey M. (Janey Malka), 1946- author

CONTENTS

Introduction	1
Child of the space race	10
Berlin – political Disneyland	34
"Irresponsible troublemakers"	36
Pushing wheelbarrows in Yugoslavia	41
"Everyone talks about the weather – not us"	45
"I always see you at revolutions"	54
Berserkeley	63
What happened to the sixties?	80
Garbage strike in Mississippi	84
Revolutionaries in suits: Japan 1971	86
I.S. in Australia: the early days	89
"Gimme your passport!": Portugal 1975	102
"We want Gough": Australia November 1975	110
I.S. in Australia: a national organisation	118
Refugee camps and Scrabble: Lebanon and Palestine 1980	136
I.S. in Australia: the 1980s	145
Mines and mass rallies: Latin America 1985	157
I.S. in Australia: Socialist Action 1985-89	177
May Day: Philippines 1987	185
Market socialism in Poland and Russia 1989	190
An inspiring revolutionary: South Korea 1991	198
I.S. in Australia: the 1990s	201
Eyewitness to mass struggle: Indonesia 1993-2001	205
Writing books	218
I.S. in Australia: taking stock	224
A life worth living	227
The highway is for gamblers	230

INTRODUCTION

The past is not dead. It is not even past.

– **William Faulkner**

The past is a foreign country: they do things differently there.

– **L.P. Hartley**

A memoir is by definition about the past. Sometimes our past selves seem very strange; it can be hard to understand why we did what we once did. But as Faulkner says, the past lives on in us today – and I think this brings us closer to the truth. Marx says something similar in his famous phrase about the past weighing "like a nightmare on the brains of the living". He was talking about social relations. But the individual, the personality of the individual and the development of individual human beings also play a role.

In his political writings, Tom has generally been reluctant to divert attention from his main arguments by introducing too personal a note. But now, Tom has decided that it is time to write more about his personal experiences. This is partly because his comrades constantly ask to hear more of his stories. But just as visiting another country adds to the understanding of what you can read about it, revisiting the country of your lived experiences adds to the knowledge that is passed on.

Tom has chosen the title for his memoir from Bob Dylan's "It's all over now, baby blue". He charts his

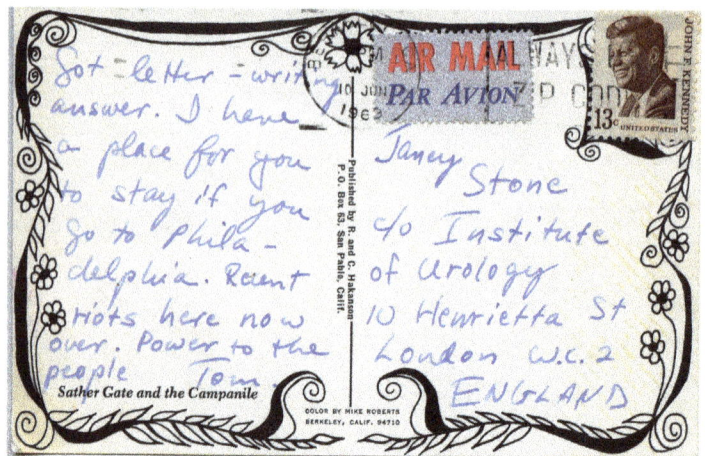

Postcard from Tom to Janey mid-1969 showing Sather Gate and the Campanile on the Berkeley campus, with psychadelic decorations

political journey along the "highway for gamblers" – from his initial introduction to a picket line with his mother while a young boy, through his growing awareness of the world as a teenager, political engagement as a student in the sixties, building a revolutionary organisation in Australia in the 1970s, 80s and 90s, and travel to many countries in Asia, Europe and the Americas. Although the focus is his life as a revolutionary socialist, the memoir fills out the personal story a little as well. This family background may not have obvious or direct connections to his life as an adult, but for the reader it add to the understanding of what makes up Tom as a person. The travel experiences told in this book all have a political dimension. But the glimpses into the more personal aspects of being a revolutionary, of travel and being exposed to other cultures, adds to the descriptions and analyses.

This book is not an autobiography. It does not contain in-depth analyses of the political or personal topics it covers. The text and the graphics are presented chronologically but otherwise there is no attempt to create an overall structure. Perhaps we can think of it as a scrapbook – a collection of stories, vignettes, anecdotes, jottings, photos, ephemera; memories that give us a taste of one person's political life. This scrapbook nonetheless reveals a lot about Tom's conception of the life he has lived. Having read the story in the earlier chapters, by the time one reads "A life worth living" there is to some degree the reckoning to be expected from an autobiography.

What's more, Tom's particular story and the many graphics also give a broader picture of social reality in the second half of the twentieth century.

A political life

Tom was born in California in 1947, the son of Evelyn (née Mann) and Robert (Bob) O'Lincoln (born Herbert Wiens). He grew up in Walnut Creek, a dormitory town east of San Francisco, and attended Las Lomas High School, Diablo Valley College and the University of California, Berkeley. He also spent two separate years as an exchange student in Germany. The first was his last year of high school, 1964-65,

which he spent in Gaggenau, near Baden. During this, his first extended time away from home, Tom expanded his horizons significantly. He spoke German at school and talked French with another exchange student living with his host family.

His experiences on his second sojourn in Germany in 1967-68, at the University of Göttingen in Lower Saxony, had a major impact on the direction of his life. Tom was radicalised and became an activist and a Marxist. He spent the summer of 1968 backpacking around Europe. That year I was doing the same. Our meeting was an accident, yet it changed the course of our lives, and subsequently the development of revolutionary organisations in Australia.

After I joined him in the US in September 1969, we got an apartment in Oakland and became members of the Berkeley branch of the recently formed International Socialists. In November 1971, we came to Australia and the following year became involved in revolutionary politics. While the social and political circumstances of the period constrained what was possible, our individual experiences and personalities also contributed to the outcomes. We introduced a particular interpretation of revolutionary Marxism here; the group we established, which consisted at its smallest point of six people, could well have sunk without trace.

The group did however get off the ground – the initial Marxist Workers Group became Socialist Workers Action Group at the end of 1972 and then the International Socialists at the end of 1975.

During the downturn of the 1980s, disputes over how best to respond led to a split, with Tom and I and a group of others leaving the IS to form Socialist Action during 1985. The two groups remerged in 1989 to form the International Socialist Organisation. Tom joined the leadership of the ISO, but withdrew from national leadership in 1992. After further disputes, Tom left the ISO and joined Socialist Alternative in 2003. He remains an active member to this day.

The five sections of this book entitled "Revolutionary Socialism in Australia" cover the development of the organisations and Tom's political activities over that period.

Tom was a leader in our revolutionary current in Australia for 20 years. He continued political activity as a rank and file member for another decade and beyond. In that time he influenced many people. One was Rick Kuhn, who paid tribute to Tom at an event in 2016:

> I first met Tom in a seedy flat that he and Janey shared in Sydney in 1976. They had inveigled a friend of mine who was an activist for courses in political economy at Sydney University, which I was also involved in, to speak to the branch. Tom has been involved in revolutionary politics since the 1960s. His writings reflect that commitment to political activity. This is not simply high theory for its own sake. It is ideas that are useful and related to our efforts to improve the planet by getting rid of capitalism.
>
> Tom played an incredibly important role in my life. I was some young undergraduate and then a graduate schmuck who knew very little about the world, who did know that what was in Russia wasn't real socialism. Tom played a role in developing me politically and in taking me seriously, which I was pretty amazed by. And he has played that role with generations of socialists in Australia.

Language and literature

When I first met Tom, he was more interested in developing his politics than in family history. But later in life it meant more to him. Some of this comes through in an unpublished account of a visit with Jane Tovey to Fresno, California, in 2012 to see his aunt Linda, who was by then nearly 98 years old. At dinner, Tom's cousin Delbert Wiens commented that "Tom belongs to a particular ethnic group" whose peculiarities might need explanation.

Tom writes:

> I'd never thought of myself as belonging to an ethnic group, unless transplanted Americans count. But in my little world, Fresno and the region south of it is Mennonite Central. Ever since I was a boy I've known about Mennonites.

Tom then refers to Delbert's articles about the transitions and upheavals that the Mennonite community went through in the New World, much of which centred on the German language,

> (which) was once fundamental to the Mennonites' identity, despite the fact that they don't come from Germany. I understood this only in the most superficial terms until I went to see my aunt. Unsure if she remembered me I mentioned a common, fond memory: that I had written her letters from Germany. Did she want to talk German with me for old times' sake?
>
> She replied: *Danke sagen auf Deutsch*. Let's say grace in German.

Delbert notes "they could not pray in English". According to Tom, close to death, his aunt "reached deep to find a language much as a Catholic might use Latin".

Tom recognised that this background had influenced him. Perhaps the biggest impact was his life-long interest in German language and literature. He not only read Hegel and Marx in the original, but was also fascinated by writers such as Thomas Mann. As early as 1967, he noted in his travel diary that he was reading a Mann collection and Günter Grass's *Dog Years*, as a result of which, he says, "the old inimitable Grass style" crept into his writing.

Tom's engagement with literature enriched his appreciation of Marxism and political theory, of history and of the world. In an unpublished essay on Faust, he commented:

> Great literature is valuable even if it's written by bilious right wingers. A famous example is the work of Balzac. His portraits of a society in which class, money and ambition are the key players have been valued by critics of left wing and right wing political persuasions. Friedrich Engels wrote that he had "learned more [from Balzac] than from all the professional historians, economists and statisticians put together".

Over several decades, Tom travelled through Asia, Europe, and Latin America, developing his skills and expanding his knowledge. When we visited Peru, he was reading in Spanish about the Peruvian Marxist Jose-Carlos Mariátegui. This involved political writings, but it was still an engagement with the language beyond having discussions with activists. Around the time of visiting Russia in 1989, he brushed up his Russian and translated "Answers from a historian" by Yuri Afanasiev.

Particularly remarkable is Tom's engagement with Indonesian language and literature. For most activists in his situation and at his age at the time (he was in his fifties) gaining a working knowledge of the language would probably have been enough. When writing the Indonesian language newsletter *Suara Socialis*, he had enough collaborators to correct errors. But this did not satisfy Tom.

As well as translating socialist books, he read and wrote about Indonesian literature. I remember him pursuing colloquial expression with dogged determination and Fleur Taylor comments that "Tom was humble about his command of Indonesian slang, but he was streets ahead of most foreigners".

Acknowledgements

Tom was a prolific writer. Unfortunately, he was diagnosed with Parkinson's disease several years ago and found it increasingly difficult to continue the creative process. I therefore stepped in to help produce this book, which has been drawn from a number of sources. Although I have had a significant role in selecting, editing and drafting material for this book, Tom has edited, rewritten and reviewed everything. This is his memoir.

Its core is a 34-page draft that Tom wrote in early 2015. To supplement the draft, there were nine oral recording sessions. I also drew on a range of material written by Tom, including published articles, internal documents, letters, unpublished

Janey and Tom in Tom's parents' house Walnut Creek 1969; (opposite page) Tom's aunt Linda, Janey, Helen Rosenberg with Tom in back row at centre, Fresno California 1983

draft essays, pamphlets and vignettes from his Red Sites website, and articles on the Marxist Interventions website that he and Rick Kuhn ran for some years. I also used memorabilia Tom kept from his travels, old diaries, letters and postcards to his family and me and a large pile of ephemera I discovered in a box in my garage. My job was to weave all this disparate material as smoothly as possible into a readable whole.

Many people have contributed to this work. Robert Zocchi recorded and transcribed the oral interviews. Without Robert's efforts, the entire project would have foundered. Liz Ross contributed much useful information relating to the chapters about the travels she did with Tom and other sections, and provided very thought-provoking comments on the draft as a whole; she also fielded many emails from me regarding dates, places and events. Joel Geier participated in the recording session on the Berkeley IS. Rick Kuhn's detailed comments and suggestions on a restructure of the draft contributed significantly to the final version. Tess Lee Ack and Fleur Taylor both contributed comment and also both proof read and copy-edited to create a quality final version. Viktoria Ivanova's brilliant cover design and layout have given the book an exciting and vibrant appearance.

Max Lane, Ian Rintoul, Graham Willett, Mick Armstrong, Sandra Bloodworth, Diane Fieldes and many others helped with dating, clarifying, translating, identifying and in many other ways, and contributed to my goal of making the book as accurate as possible.

Tom's cousins in the US also provided input. Linda Cheever scanned and sent me letters from Tom's parents to his aunt and uncle from the 1940s, 50s and 60s, which Tom himself had never previously seen. Marj Wiens, Judi Hahnel, Char McLaughlin and Larry Robinson answered a number of questions and clarified a number of points about early family history and also provided photos.

Throughout most of the time that this book was being written, Jane Tovey was helping and supporting Tom in many ways.

Even the editor of a book sometimes needs an editor and Ben Hillier played that role for me. His feedback and insights sustained me through the creative process.

Lastly I would like to thank Tom himself, for doing his best despite his illness to write and produce a worthwhile book. Tom has retained his ability as an editor, in particular his ability to improve a text by shortening it. I am one of the many people who learned to write from him, and I continued to learn while working on this book. Throughout the last 18 months, he graciously put up with me probing his life and his memories. It has been a pleasure to work on this project.

Tom has been my political mentor since we got together in 1969. He was my partner for nearly 20 years, and since then one of my closest friends. Throughout, I have looked to Tom for guidance and comment in my writing and in my political involvement.

Working on this project has been a unique experience. Discovering Tom's old travel diaries, reading his old letters to me and reliving our shared experiences have reminded me how much he enriched my life. This book is my gift to you, Tom, for having been there.

Janey Stone
March 2017

Dear Betty & Herold -

    Just a short note to announce the arrival of Thomas O'Lincoln last evening, August 27, weighing 8 pounds 9 ounces, and stretching 21 inches from stem to stem.

    Passage was a bit stormy, due to his large size & her small size, also his head was a bit too far aft, so that a bit of assistance with forceps was needed. Also rather lengthy, commencing at midnite Monday - Tuesday, and arriving Wednesday evening.

    However, all is well. Saw her this afternoon, and she looked fine, and says she feels O.K.

    I have also recovered and am fast returning to normal.

                Love,
                     Bob.

Tom (right) and Terry, studio photo early 1950s. Growing up in California, Tom once asked his father whether they could "go out West"

CHILD OF THE SPACE RACE

On 28 August 1947, Robert O'Lincoln wrote a letter to his brother and sister-in-law, Herold and Betty Wiens:

> Just a short note to announce the arrival of Thomas O'Lincoln last evening, Aug 27, weighing 8 pounds 9 ounces, and stretching 21 inches from stem to stern. Passage was a bit stormy, due to his large size and her small size… Also rather lengthy, commencing midnite Monday-Tuesday and arriving Wednesday evening. However all is well. Saw her this afternoon and she looked fine. I have also recovered and am fast returning to normal.

In this letter, my father's use of nautical terms reveals his naval background, and the tone his ironic sense of humour.

I grew up in Walnut Creek in Contra Costa county, about 34 km east of San Francisco, past the Berkeley Hills. Contra Costa is a county of towns spread through a countryside of rolling hills and rural scenes. Walnut Creek began its white history as a number of properties granted to Spanish settlers, one of whom named his ranch *Arroyo de las Nueces* (Creek of the Walnuts). After enough bloodshed to secure California for American settlers from the east, it continued as an American township and got its first post office in 1862. When I was growing up in the 1950s, Walnut Creek was surrounded by cows and grassy fields and the occasional rattle-snake. School kids came to school with blackened palms during the walnut harvest. Behind

the grade school stood Shell Ridge, full of fossils; and like all California grade school pupils I travelled to school every morning in a yellow bus, just like in *The Simpsons*.

Gradually Walnut Creek morphed into what Americans call a suburb, a town not far from a metropolitan area which acts to a degree as a dormitory town. But it was not yet a big town when I was growing up: although the population quadrupled following the opening downtown of the county's first major retail centre in 1951, it was still under 10,000 in 1960.

I suppose in some ways I had an idyllic childhood. As a small boy I was "Tommy" to my parents. My mother wrote in her letters to Herold and Betty about my early development:

> (Tommy is) at that "getting into everything" stage and nothing is safe from his clutching hands.
>
> Tommy is going through a no-no stage which seems to be lasting a long, long time…. (He) is very shy with strangers and extremely noisy and talkative at home. He eats like a truck driver though. Our only trouble is having enough food for him.

My parents built their own house on the outskirts of Walnut Creek, at the end of the road and with open fields behind it, where my brother and I played in the typical manner of the 1950s, when children roamed more freely. The building of this house was a feature of my childhood. In a letter to Herold and Betty my mother wrote:

> Bob of course is sawing and hammering constantly. So perhaps before too many years we'll have a complete house.

My parents put an enormous

Tom and Terry (in the wheelbarrow) in the yard behind their house on the edge of Walnut Creek; Tom, early 1950s

amount of energy into that house, and when they were later forced to sell it they felt the loss bitterly.

The first thing that strikes the visitor to Walnut Creek is that it is white – it was overwhelmingly white when I was growing up and remains so today. It looks squeaky clean and middle class – a bit like the more old-fashioned sitcoms. There were and still are few footpaths – you were expected to drive. For example, I might see an ad for Coca-Cola and get a craving for it, so I would get into the car and drive to the liquor store. Complete car culture, classic Americana.

Perhaps the first Black person I ever met was during a visit in the late 1950s to Pittsburgh, a steel town in the eastern part of Contra Costa county, which was named after the big city in Pennsylvania. Pittsburgh CA was effectively segregated – not legally, but certainly so in actual fact.

My father had dropped me off somewhere in the town, and told me to amuse myself for the day. I ran into a Black youth who was equally bored and looking for something to do. He said, "Do you want to play booty bust?" "Booty bust" was played with a basketball: if you shot the basket and were successful you got a point, but if you missed it then the other person got to throw the basketball at your bum as hard as possible. Classic Americana, Pittsburgh style!

In a different way, Las Lomas High School was classic Americana too. Apart from a few Chinese, the student population was pretty white. The wrestling coach was Mexican. Looking for him one day I was told "It's this big Mexican guy, you'll recognise him." – this alone made him distinctive. The student parking lot was far larger than the one for the staff, and there were older kids in letter sweaters. To get a letter sweater was the badge of the alpha male, ideally gained for starring at football. I played a number of sports, including ice-hockey. One of the PE teachers kept reminding me I was capable of lettering in cross-country running. I desperately wanted a letter, but I wondered if a Senior year full of unpleasant running around town was worth the price. I decided it wasn't, after watching the Lettermen carry on. They would never have let me into their macho club anyway.

That was the small world of the teenager. In the wider world, the fifties was the time of the Cold War and the space race, both of which had quite an impact on me. I tried to capture the atmosphere of this period in an article I wrote in 2006 after seeing the BBC TV series, *Space Race*.

Child of the Space Race

October 2006, published online at Tom O'Lincoln's Red Sites [slightly edited]

Watching Space Race was a mad time-warp. Curious memories sprang from nowhere. I had grown up in Wernher von Braun's America, and suddenly it all came back.[1]

They were times of hope and fear. Hope that science was a force for good, embodied in the quest to send a Man Into Space; and fear that the Soviets would beat us to it, which was a terrible prospect because science had also emerged as the great destroyer. For all the talk of peace the space race and the arms race were inseparable, because rockets could deliver payloads, so control of space was above all a military necessity for Moscow and Washington. Why else so much gnashing of American teeth over Sputnik?

In 1969 I would go out into the street and gaze up at the moon, as thrilled as von Braun on TV, imagining Neil Armstrong up there walking around. But as a little boy in the early fifties I had three nightmares about nuclear war; enough to plague my parents with worry. Dreams a bit like those in Bob Dylan's "Talkin' World War III Blues".

They got their start in school. This was a place to hear exhilarating tales about satellite launches (except when they blew up), and at the same time a stage for paranoid war games. Daily science classes dwelt on the space race, and each morning the classroom loudspeakers blared out the national anthem and the "Pledge to Our Flag". (Blech. Yet I can also smile, remembering how some wag in the back row would call out "Play ball!" after the anthem, just like at the baseball games.)

Then one day the speakers came to life in the middle of the day, bringing us a test run for Conelrad, the clunky round-robin radio system designed to shift signals from one transmitter to another before the Russian rockets could home in on any fixed broadcast. Awkward voices scratched clichés to us through the static, in that pompous fifties announcer style: "This is the Voice of Conelrad". Bob Dylan recalled it with fitting irony:

Well, I remember seein' some ad,
So I turned on my Conelrad.

*But I didn't pay my Con Ed bill,
So the radio didn't work so well.*

No, it didn't work well at all, I can confirm that.

Another time the whole school marched home in an evacuation drill, my contingent trooping along the railway tracks. Back at home my dad was building a house on a slope from concrete blocks. The under-story formed a spacious basement, which could serve as a bomb shelter. Or at least that's what the neighbours brightly announced. Why, it would add value to the house. Later Dylan made me wonder how we might have behaved if we had ever put it to use:

*Well, I rung the fallout shelter bell
And I leaned my head and I gave a yell,
Give me a string bean, I'm a hungry man.
A shotgun fired and away I ran.
I don't blame them too much though,
I know I look funny.*

A talented boy at my school wrote a play on this same theme: a family in their shelter with some fearful spectre knocking on the door. The private bomb shelter was a study in social alienation. But we had to stop the Communists, didn't we? By the time of the 1962 missile crisis, I did scratch up enough original thought to ask why America got to decide whether Cuba had missiles. After all, America had secured them without asking anyone. Why couldn't Castro join the space race too? My mother told me sharply that we had to stop the Communists. Temporarily convinced, I joined a school excursion to the local missile base.

Yes, no bullshit, that's where we went. Can't you just see us schoolboys at a missile base? Awesome.

Some of the boys thought the air force should shoot off a rocket, just so we could watch. They wanted the Wernher von Braun experience. The military guide shook his head; then he condescendingly asked if we knew why the answer was no. I guessed: "What goes up must come down?" Yeah that too, he laughed, before getting to the main reason: these rockets cost like a million dollars each.

So what, it was worth it to stop the Communists.

It took a war in Vietnam to shake me up. Forget nobility or logic, at the start this was all about naked self-preservation. I'd been vaguely pro-war until I realised I could be sent off to die, and then my ideas started to change. Slowly I ditched the bomb shelter mentality, the space race craze, the Conelrad mindset. The Communists became fellow human beings, and in a growing movement against the war I discovered a curious new thing called solidarity. Like that Dylan guy said:

I'll let you be in my dreams if I can be in yours.

Tom, Evelyn (Tom's mother), Terry, Stanley Mann (Tom's maternal uncle), Theresa Mann (Tom's maternal grandmother); Tom playing ice hockey, mid 1960s; Tom (left) and Terry (kneeling) with Tom's dog Red in the yard behind their house on the edge of Walnut Creek, early 1950s

Bob-o'-link, bob-o'-link

There have only really been five people with the name O'Lincoln: my parents, my brother and myself; later Janey Stone gained the name (legally) when she and I got married. The name is actually a semantic nonsense as the prefix "O'" is Celtic, but Lincoln is English; before us there was no such name. So where did it come from?

My father was born Herbert (Bert) Wiens in 1908. His parents, Frank and Agnes Wiens, were German-speaking Mennonites, one of the groups belonging to the Christian Anabaptist denominations, which also includes the Amish. Their Mennonite grouping had originated in the 19th century in what was then part of the Russian Empire but today is in the Ukraine. My great-grandparents emigrated in the late 1870s and settled in Nebraska, where my grandfather F. J. Wiens was born. Frank showed much promise as an "evangelist" – he was sometimes called the Billy Sunday of the Mennonites in the prairie states after a famous American evangelist of the early 20th century. My aunt Adina described him in her book of family history, as "preaching repentance and forgiveness of sins in persuasive German, with an occasional revival meeting in English to recapture the defectors". My grandmother Agnes Harder Wiens was also well respected in the community.

In 1910, my grandparents set out for China to be missionaries, taking my father, then a small boy, with them. They travelled by way of Russia, where they spent some time with their extended family in the home village Sparrau in the Molotschna

Colony in Russia, founded in 1804 by Mennonite settlers from West Prussia. Here my aunt Adina was born, and my grandfather proselytised to large audiences. A year later, having travelled on the Trans-Siberian Railway via Manchuria to Vladivostok on the southeast coast of Russia, then by boat, they arrived in Shanghai on 9 October 1911. It was coincidentally the day that the Chinese declared independence from the Manchu dynasty.

After various adventures, the Wiens family established a mission compound in Shanghang in Fujian province where my father spent his early years.

It's not clear how many Chinese welcomed my ancestors' Bible lore. Some really did take to it; others were "rice Christians", who would rather pray than starve. The missionaries had rice.

Life for my father and his brothers and sisters in Shanghang was good; they were cared for by loving Chinese amahs and spoke Chinese.

But then a minor family tragedy unfolded in the life of little Bert Wiens. At the age of eight he was sent home alone to the US because a suitable education (as his parents saw it) wasn't obtainable in China. Later on, my family tended to be very critical of my grandfather for doing this, but this was unfair. In later years, Grandfather was clearly full of remorse. In his memoirs he writes about the departure of his son whom he called his "Little Prince":

Frank Wiens (Tom's paternal grandfather), Roland, Linda, Herbert (Tom's father), Herold, Adina, Agnes Wiens (Tom's paternal grandmother). Photo taken in China mid 1920s; (below) postcard style photo of Frank and Agnes Wiens with Herbert and Adina, Russia 1911

Herbert did not cry when we said goodbye. He has always been a stoic little character... However he gave me an extra tight hug. I, on the other hand, felt that my insides were being torn apart...

My mind followed that ship bearing my treasure over the ocean waves... *In meinem Herzen wogte es gewaltig:* In my heart were mighty storms.

Living with relatives in Hillsboro Kentucky, Bert was bullied mercilessly by his cousins and the "defenceless little boy so far from home" lived the hard life common in farming communities, a life also constrained by rigid religious customs.²

Bert was reunited with his family in 1921, when they came home on furlough, which they spent with their maternal grandparents in Hillsboro Kansas. My aunt Adina, writing later about this visit, commented: "Our time with them had been grim and humourless."³

Bert returned to China with his family in 1922, but his experiences of being torn away from his parents and then growing up in the Mennonite community embittered him. Aunt Adina writes of the "protective shell that isolated him from our family" that developed during those years.

As an act of rejection, Herbert Wiens changed his name as an adult. He chose a new name from the poem "Robert of Lincoln" by the American romantic poet, William Cullen Bryant:

Merrily swinging on briar and weed,
Near to the nest of his little dame,
Over the mountain-side or mead,
Robert of Lincoln is telling his name;
Bob-o'-link, bob-o'-link,
Spink, spank, spink;
Snug and safe in that nest of ours,
Hidden among the summer flowers.
*Chee, chee, chee.*⁴

Left to right: Tom's grandparents Frank and Agnes Wiens; Frank Wiens preaching; mission house in Shanghang; Frank Wiens and son Bert fishing. All photos taken in China

The bobolink is a small New World blackbird, with black, white and cream colouring. The poet converts its call of bob-o'-link to a name: Robert of Lincoln. I don't know what it was it that attracted my father to this poem or the bird, but it clearly had an impact on him.

For my father, changing his first name from Herbert to Robert, especially since he was generally known as Bert, did not require an enormous leap. On the other hand, the completely different surname meant a clear distancing from and rejection of both his family and his Mennonite heritage. The Wiens family were very prominent among his branch of the Mennonites, known for being community leaders, preachers and missionaries. My father rejected all of this.

Dad went on to become an electrician, then during World War II, he joined the Navy. After the war he benefitted from the GI Bill, attending the University of California Berkeley campus and becoming a teacher.

While I was growing up in the 1950s, he had trouble getting jobs close to home. At one stage he was working in Pittsburgh, California. He even looked in places like Lodi in northern California, made famous in a song by Creedence Clearwater Revival, who clearly thought it was the epitome of a boring place. Dad eventually ended up with a job near home in Concord, still a pretty suburban area, but much more gritty than Walnut Creek. But he still wasn't very happy, as he didn't enjoy teaching working class kids – he generally preferred the better behaved middle class pupils, and particularly enjoyed a program for "gifted" children he was involved in for a while

in the mid-1960s. My father felt he had moved up in rank by going into teaching, having previously been a tradesman. He called one subject he taught "bonehead maths".

In spite of, or perhaps because of, his embitterment, my father told many stories about the Mennonites and China. One story about himself concerned a river journey in a storm. Here it is as my grandfather describes it in his journal:

> At one place the swirling water caught the boat and turned it clear around so that we were headed down stream backwards. ... As the boat careened wildly through the twists and turns Herbert moved close to me and said, "Papa, surely my sins are too great!" I asked: "How so?" He then recounted all his "bad deeds", among them: "And I hit Adina every day."

Another story concerns the Mennonite objection to movies, then still a very novel form of entertainment. The Mennonites thought movies sinful and preached vociferously against them. But while he was on the ship returning to China in 1922, my grandfather chanced upon a movie screening. He sat watching this phenomenon and later commented how great it was, how useful a tool it would be in his missionary work. He didn't know that this was the very thing he had preached against.[5]

Of course, the real issue was not about the medium as such, it was really about the gathering of crowds, the sexes sitting together in the dark where anything could happen.

My father also used to tell how one of his uncles said he had been "called upon" to follow Jesus while working in the fields. And my father used to say, "He must have been working really hard in that field. It must have been really hot," implying he wanted to get out of having to do manual labour.

Robert and Evelyn O'Lincoln, around the time of their marriage in 1944; Robert early 1940s; Evelyn in her nurses' uniform early 1940s

The Irish were a lot of fun

My mother had no such family stories from the world of the Irish – or so she would resentfully say. And then she would add, "but they were a lot of fun."

But of course there *were* stories, and she did tell me some.

Mother was born Evelyn Elizabeth Mann in Minneapolis in 1910 to parents Theresa and Joseph Mann. The family was very poor. Later they moved to Rockford, Illinois, when her father got a job there. Rockford was an industrial city, with a history of socialist and unionist activism. My maternal grandfather was rather rebellious and talked of socialism. He was an Irish American - potato famine Irish, not necessarily coming to America during the famine, but influenced by that background.

My grandfather died quite young, around the age of 40. Although desperately poor, my grandmother felt she had to buy the steel coffin that the undertakers pressured her to take. My grandmother's attitude was at the opposite extreme: she had a complete indifference to what happens to the dead. This expense would have been an enormous burden to her, but fortunately my mother prevented its purchase.

My mother called her father "an ass" because he was influenced by socialist ideas and because after a major strike was lost he had to go "begging back for a job". Even if he was an ass, I think it would have been good to have known him. Many strikes have ended with workers going back begging for a job, but they're still an important part of labour history.

I never knew my maternal grandfather, but my grandmother was a significant figure in my life. She had her own stories and also photos, including from an outing to the Black Hills in South Dakota. She told of grandparents who spoke Gaelic in the New World.

Having grown up in serious poverty, my mother in later life was the kind of person who hated the idea of holding on to clothes and other possessions until the bitter end. The moment socks or underwear got a hole in them, they were thrown out. "No more darning of socks!" she said. I once had a shirt with a tear down the back. She was beside herself. "Get rid of that stupid shirt!" she exclaimed. "That's what we did in the 30s. We're not doing it now!"

On another occasion, she complained about holes in my underwear – "why don't you buy some new ones?" She despaired about my rather worn and hippyish clothing.

My mother trained as a nurse in the 1930s. She worked on the wards, studied nursing, had a place to live, and was paid a wage – it would have been a pittance, but it was a wage. At that time it was a way out for working class women when they left school, as you got paid while learning a skill.

Mother was not really aware of the Depression until she left nursing school. Nursing students then were tightly regulated. Living almost monastically in the accommodation

Evelyn O'Lincoln as a nurse early 1950s

provided, keeping rigid hours, and having to study in their spare time; there would have been little leisure. But when she came out into the world afterwards, she was shocked at the poverty.

After she finished her training, my mother worked in a major hospital in Chicago, which was a large and sophisticated city of 3 million, and hosted the World Fair 1933-34. Most intriguing to me of the stories Mother told was about the day mobster Lucky Luciano visited the ward where she was working. She gave me few details, but I am still fascinated by the thought of his companion called Greasy Thumb Guzik. This was some more classic Americana.

My mother had a boyfriend who was a Jewish doctor, and he proposed to her somewhat casually, "Hey why don't we get married?" It was just before World War II, and the future was very uncertain.

Mother did not get on very well with her husband's family due to the fact that she wasn't Jewish. Chicago actually had the third largest Jewish population in the world at the time, after New York City and Warsaw, and a large segment had moved up significantly in society since arriving around the turn of the century. Mother found her in-laws to be somewhat exclusive and selective about who got invited into the family. They were very conservative, but also looked down on her because they saw her as a provincial who didn't understand the ways of a big city like Chicago.

The marriage was not fated to last very long. Having joined the Navy, Mother's husband died when his submarine was hit by a Japanese submarine. Like many who suffered such a personal loss during the War, my mother just could not get over her feelings; she could never forgive the Japanese.

Mother married my father at the age of 34 in 1944 and they moved out to California, where she expected a different life. But she again had in-laws with a minority religion, who looked down on her, this time because she was a non-believer. Ironically, this time she was the one who felt herself more cultured; provincial Walnut Creek was a poor exchange for sophisticated and urban Chicago.

Mother was a staunch advocate of science and especially medicine. After seeing my brother die at home, she snapped, "I want to die in a hospital!" On the subject of self-indulgence she was scathing: "None of us is that important. Just the product of five minutes of fucking."

Romance of the road

Tom's brother
Terry O'Lincoln

My brother Terry was four years younger than me and a premature baby. Through most of his life, he suffered from a bowel condition. Mother was always haunted by a feeling of guilt that his illness was related to his premature birth, and was somehow her fault. Terry only lived to be 32 and died suddenly of cancer in January 1983.

Even though he died young, Terry had a very full life with a wide variety of experiences. University wasn't for him. I helped him bluff his way through the only semester he was at Berkeley, and he ended up training to be a welder.

Terry was very interested in the writer Jack Kerouac. Just think of San Francisco, the North Beach area, night clubs area, seedy – that's what Terry was attracted to. But also to being on the road, the romance of the road, which for him was really about hitchhiking or perhaps Greyhound buses. To him this was the embodiment of cool. Once he went hitchhiking on Route 66 and stayed in a place called God's Crash Pad, and he loved it. He loved the fact that there could be something in America with this ridiculous name.

I saw Terry's attitude close up when he visited Germany in 1967

26 Child of the space race

when I was living there. We arrived late in Berlin at night and had difficulty finding somewhere to stay. Terry said that had he been alone he would have just slept in the street. The main thing he wanted to see was the Brandenburg Gate, which at that time had a sort of spy novel atmosphere that he saw as cool.

When he visited Paris, Terry decided it would be cool to sleep under one of the bridges. Late at night he got held up by somebody with a knife. Fortunately he wasn't hurt as they were just after his money.

Terry was an attractive guy and had some interesting relationships with women. But he told me once that he was frustrated with the women he met in the US. "Why do they always have to be foxy?" – meaning the fakeness of it all. How many young men in their twenties are repulsed by "foxiness"?

Perhaps Terry's attitude to women was partly the product of a New Left environment that was all around him. Certainly he loved the *Berkeley Barb* newspaper – not because of its political content as such, but because by instinct he was rebellious.

Terry often acted completely spontaneously. One day in 1973, when I was living in Melbourne, I found a letter from him waiting for me when I returned from a short trip, saying he was in Australia. I telegrammed my parents: "Terry in Australia or joke?" I got a reply saying: "Yes he's there, he just didn't want to bother you." He eventually did turn up in Melbourne, having hitchhiked from North Queensland, where he was driven mad by flies because he didn't know about insect repellent. He had also been threatened by a gang of thugs, but fortunately he had learnt karate.

An even more surprising encounter occurred when Janey and I were in Penang in 1975. I was walking down a hotel corridor when I heard a voice behind me, "Tom, are you here?" I turned around and there was Terry, completely out of the blue. He knew we were travelling in South East Asia, but had not bothered to contact us.

We sent a joint postcard home:

Tom: Hi there, heh, heh. I was walking along and who should I meet but – guess who. This is ridiculous. But please save this postcard as a souvenir, because I won't believe it later.

Terry: What's happening? Tom didn't believe it. He thought I was playing a mean joke on him. Maybe I'll go to India and freak him at the Taj Mahal.

Terry's relaxed attitude when travelling shows clearly in some unpublished travel notes he wrote about a trip to Europe with a workmate called Mike in 1980. They started out in Lisbon, which Terry liked:

Unfortunately Mike injured himself there. We stayed at the Whiskey Bar until 2.00 am and came back to the hostel in an absolute hell bound state and found we were locked out. Imagine, second night of the trip, and we're locked out in the street, drunk, freezing, at 2.00 am. We took a shit in the Sheraton Hotel and almost got arrested...we went back to the hostel, where Mike climbed over the fence into the courtyard, and that's where he hurt his knee...(but) the back door was locked. We spent the night in the subway.

Madrid was our next stop. An equally ridiculous and sad event happened there. We were all asleep at the hostel, when, about midnight, one of the people running the place turns on the light and brings in another traveller. All the beds are full. Apparently one of the people in our room was under the impression he'd reserved a bed for three days. We argued and argued with the owner, as he wouldn't let the man stay. He wouldn't let him sleep on the floor. As I'd been out on the street a couple of nights before, I was pissed off, so I joined in the squabbling. I was also drunk so I probably did more harm than good. We locked the owner out at one point but he had a key. He threatened to call the police, so we quietened down and the man left with his pack.

We still weren't ready to let our fellow traveller sleep in the street, so we tied sheets together and hung them out the window to the street below. It didn't work at first. The sheets tore about twenty feet up and the man fell, breaking his ankle. We tried again, and got him up the second time. The next morning he sneaked out quietly.

Terry later visited Indonesia:

I was quite famous around Java. In Jogjakarta I was "Mr Stoned" and in Semarang I was "Blug Blug"...

In Jakarta, the bar girls called me "Satu Lagi". It means "one more" in Indonesian. I could always be found in the plastic, pitch dark massage bars (night clubs they had the nerve to call them) ... There I'd sit in the early afternoon, happy, lit up, and finally slobbering drunk, calling out "Satu lagi" like a battle cry.

Early political experiences

Although my parents were not really political, some incidents in my childhood set the scene for my later development.

One day when I was about 10, my mother and I were walking past a picket line in front of a Safeway store in Walnut Creek. I asked her, "What's that?" She said, "That's a picket line, so we mustn't shop there." I said "But we can go in there if we want to?" "Yes, but they're asking people to stay out. What they're doing there is important." She sensed that picket lines mattered.

Mother's experience with her own nurses' union however led to her feeling quite frustrated. The union conducted disputes by getting everyone to resign, because of course nurses "don't go on strike". Having written resignation letters, once the strike was over, you had to withdraw the resignation, which was a humiliating experience.

My father's experience with unions also led to frustration. In the 1950s he worked for PG&E (Pacific Gas and Electricity Company) in California and was a member of the electricians' union. My father was not very political; his main role as a unionist seems to have been antagonising the foreman. Eventually after an incident he was demoted and then lost his job. Not only did this affect his attitude to unionism, it also had a major impact on my home environment. We had to sell our house and in order to buy another one, my mother went back to work, on night shifts. She resented the whole situation.

Dad was aware of her resentment. He commented in a letter in 1964,

Remembering the 1964 Republican National Convention

Tom O'Lincoln

It was June 1964 in San Francisco. Republicans were streaming into town. They were to meet at the aptly named Cow Palace.

So were we – the demonstrators. We had taken on the seemingly heartless task of keeping Barry Goldwater out of the White House.

Goldwater was an ultra-conservative and had sworn to use nuclear weapons and decisively escalate the war in Vietnam. The presidential primaries were over, and he was the presumptive nominee. The hard Republican right declared, "In your heart, you know he's right".

The liberals replied, "In your guts, you know he's nuts". But it was scant consolation.

Down on the convention floor, I was making a discovery. The anti-Goldwater forces of the party had apparently opened the doors to Cow Palace and thrown away the keys.

I led a few chants and waved my placard around. This in turn got me on TV.

The anti-Goldwater forces were pushing for the nomination of governor William Scranton of Pennsylvania. Still full of excitement, I went down to the Scranton headquarters to stuff envelopes –the start of a scurrilous rumour that I was once a member of the young Republicans.

The Scranton push failed and Goldwater was officially nominated. He went on to get thrashed in the election by Lyndon Johnson.

> Five years later I joined a revolutionary organisation. I never looked back.

Relieved, I scribbled in my diary: "Goldwater is destroyed". But he wasn't. LBJ sent half a million troops to lay waste to Vietnam.

The demonstrators went on to bigger things.

What did I accomplish, enrolling in a liberal capitalist campaign? To stuff envelopes. But five years later I joined a revolutionary organisation. There I learned to organise against the bosses. I never looked back.

Red Flag 13 June 2016

"Evelyn's work is…a constant physical and nervous strain. I really marvel at her ability to continue so long at it."

My own first political experience probably was attending a civil rights picket line in the early 1960s when I was 13 or 14 and at high school.

I also remember many happy school hours spent drafting a letter to my congressman, making the time-worn argument for scrapping the Electoral College, a peculiarity of the American electoral system which biases the presidential vote towards the smaller states. (This is how Donald Trump won the 2016 presidential race while Hillary Clinton got the popular vote.) My congressman wrote back, just as he did every year, with a standard letter, all about a token bill he entered every year which sank without a trace. The vested interests in the small states would not tolerate a change.

Then I got involved in activities around the 1964 Republican Convention. I went door to door, and licked envelopes in an effort to stop-right winger Barry Goldwater from getting nominated for president. Like a lot of Americans, I feared Goldwater's militarism, seeing Lyndon Johnson as the peace candidate. Within a year of the election, Johnson had dispatched half a million troops to Vietnam. Above is an item I wrote for *Red Flag* in 2016 about that experience.

Why German?

I think all my friends know I speak German. But, why German? It started with my family background.

The first foreign language I was exposed to as a child was Chinese. As young children in China, my father and his siblings had spoken Hakka Chinese, having attended the mission school with local children. Later, Dad and my Aunt Linda invented this little nonsense rhyme which he taught to me.

Malika tsing
Nyao lika cha
Dzulika dzing teo
A yung go szz

The words don't mean anything, but for me they were a fascinating link into another culture.

When I was 13 my father began teaching me German. My cousin Delbert Wiens wrote about the importance of the German language to the Mennonites, both culturally and as the bearer of their religion.

> As far as they were concerned, the Scriptures were written in German. Even those who knew about the Greek and Hebrew found that fact profoundly irrelevant…they simply took for granted that they shared their cultural language with the biblical peoples.[6]

My father was imbued with this feeling, even though he had rejected the religion. He still fell into German on certain occasions, for instance, ending a letter to his brother written in English with "*Nu, ich bin zu Ende des Papiers, also Auf Wiedersehen!*"

(Well, I'm at the end of the paper, so good bye!).

We didn't think of the German language as a heritage until decades later, but it was an unexpected open door. In high school I started French, which I used in real life on my first visit as an exchange student to Germany, where a young French woman was also a guest in my host family. I also studied French at university.

When I first came to Australia, I taught French at Maribyrnong High School in Melbourne's west. The kids converted the sounds of French, "*un, deux, trois*" into Australian "ahn, der, twa". A group of immigrant children from France arrived at the school. Because I found the school assemblies boring, I was able to get out of them by teaching these French students, in French, about things to do with Australia – what is the capital, what are the cities, writing a few essays and so on. After a few weeks, the principal realised I was avoiding his assemblies and made me bring the French students along.

At university, I briefly focused on Russian as a career direction. I started out with the idea that there was going to be a ramping up of the Cold War, and "we had to defeat Communism", and I thought in order to do so the US would need language specialists. As part of this approach, I subscribed to an East German newspaper. So I saw a whole career ahead of me, using both the Russian language and my knowledge of Eastern bloc politics.

But it turned out it not to be so easy. I had more trouble with Russian than with any other language, but very quickly it also became obvious that Russian was not going to provide me with a career, as I was swept into left wing politics. I let the language drift and did nothing about it for a couple of decades. I only picked it up again when Gorbachev came to power, and events in Russia were drawing renewed attention.

I have always been generally interested in languages and linguistics. A book that influenced me was *Language in Thought and Action*. The author, S.I. Hayakawa, was Canadian-born of Japanese ancestry, and he became President of San Francisco State College.[7] I was fascinated to learn about the common patterns in language and also felt a broad desire to speak to everyone in their native language, so much so that it became obsessive.

Learning a foreign language is like a window. Open the window and you see the world out there. Being able to speak languages gives you experienc-

Tom's grandfather Frank Wiens wrote his book *Pioneer work among the Hakkas of South China* in German

es you would otherwise never have.

But that was later. Having found German easy, and having started early, I got straight As. The easiest way to go on getting good marks was to go on doing German, which I did relentlessly. I was genuinely interested in German and in visiting Germany. But once politics came on the scene, doing something that was easy also left me plenty of time for politics. The two came together during my time in Germany as an exchange student.

Child of the space race

BERLIN – POLITICAL DISNEYLAND

The years I spent studying in Germany marked directions for the rest of my life. My first visit was during the last year of high school in 1964-65, which I spent as an exchange student in Gaggenau in south-west Germany near Baden.

The nature of travel in those days is reflected in a letter from my father to Herold and Betty.

> We saw Tom off from San Francisco at 10.30 Saturday, Aug 22 and he arrived in Frankfurt at 8.30 Sunday morning, a flight of fifteen hours, with refuelling stops in Montreal at 6.00 pm and London at 6.00 am.

Although I had "faithfully promised" to write as soon as I arrived, two weeks later my parents were still waiting for a letter from me. My father wrote in his letter, "As a fellow teacher said the other day, 'Show me a teenager who can write!'." Eventually they gave in to their anxiety and rang me: the call cost $12.

My experience in Gaggenau was not very political – I was only 17, and the mass student movement was still to come. But I do remember the Italian *Gastarbeiter* (guest workers), who lived there isolated from their families as there stay was seen as temporary. Some of the German kids said derogatory things about the Italians. I was already liberalised, and was aware of racism and xenophobia, so I didn't agree with them.

But what became an intensely political experience was Berlin. I was captivated by this city, which I found the most intriguing anywhere, because of the ideological conflicts surrounding it in the 1960s. For me there were few places more fascinating than the double city, especially as I had a pen pal *drüben* (over there), as most people in West Germany called East Germany.

It was the height of the Cold War, not long after the Wall was built, but in any case I was intrigued by the idea that there was someplace that was different, a challenge to the system.

There were a number of crossing points to the East, such as the famous Checkpoint Charlie, with the signs "You are leaving the American Sector". Americans had a semi-automatic right to go to East Berlin because of the occupation. You just walked across, they checked your passport and that was it. You had to change a minimum amount of money, but you couldn't change any back, so it was a type of tax. My East Berlin pen-pal Sophie and I called it the *Eintritt* (admission fee).

For me the idea of East Berlin was a sort of a Disneyland. The reality was different. Having got there for the first time, I didn't know what to do with myself. You go across to the other side of the wall, and unless you've got some plan, what do you do when you get there? Walk around, look at the buildings, say "That looks boring", and go back to West Berlin where all the action is. That's what most people did, and so did I.

I wrote an account of this trip to Berlin for the high school paper, but was pretty lax in writing to my parents about it, which my father complained about again.

> He has not been a very satisfactory correspondent, and I can well understand, now, how my own parents felt about me as a correspondent. The things parents want to hear about are NOT the ones teenage boys usually consider the most important items of news! So we have gotten a lot of what we consider garbage, and not very much of the vital news.

Dad did foresee some benefit to me from my travels in Europe, commenting that I "should not be a provincial" by the time I returned. At the end of the school year in April, the Latin teacher took the class to Rome and then I travelled round Europe for several weeks. My father obligingly gave my itinerary in a letter: Rome April 2-13. Heidelberg April 15-17, Munich April 18-20, Chiemsee April 21-23. "From then to June we have nothing but a big fat blank." My father opined that "after all this he will probably consider Walnut Creek quite tame".

"IRRESPONSIBLE TROUBLEMAKERS"

Prosperity in post-war America seemed to have solved the problem of getting a reasonable job, and an intellectual community would provide a life based on liberal values. Great hopes were vested in a liberal education. Precisely this is what so many parents wanted to provide, and to achieve it in northern California they sent their children to study at Berkeley. But in 1964, something happened they didn't anticipate and many didn't like. The Free Speech Movement (FSM) was the biggest student mobilisation of its type in the US up until then, so it was fitting that it also drew the largest police mobilisation.

Many of the activists had gone south in the summer Freedom Rides. On returning to campus in September 1964 they discovered that the administration they had admired was not on their side. University President Clark Kerr did everything he could to keep free expression within bounds the students found intolerable.

Who were the leaders of the FSM? They were irresponsible troublemakers, according to Evelyn and Robert O'Lincoln of Walnut Creek, California. My dad was scathing in the letter he sent to me in Gaggenau, West Germany, where I was at school. But the letter came with clippings from the *San Francisco Chronicle* that made the furious student actions look good to me. A lot of people thought the same as my parents did. But *Life* magazine columnist Shana Alexander got a closer look:

> The FSMers I met were all serious students, idealists...passionate about

Free Speech Movement executive committee meeting in Berkeley, October 1964. Joel Geier at centre with hand to head, Mario Savio speaking and Jerry Rubin front right. Photo: Joel Geier

civil rights. Although, regrettably, they never dress nor sound one bit like Martin Luther King, they do feel like him.[8]

My father had sent the clippings, thinking I'd look at them and think "Isn't this terrible!" In fact my reaction was, "Oh, that's interesting." I wasn't very politicised yet, but I did take up the argument against my father. By the time I got back to America, Berkeley had a bad name. People said to me "You don't want to go there, do you?"

Having been in Germany, I missed the required course in civics normally taken in the last year of high school. Although I would pull out my American civics text and study it while travelling in the train around Europe, upon my return I was too late to qualify to get into Berkeley. So I spent my first tertiary year at Diablo Valley College (DVC) away from the action.

At one point however, after the police broke up an anti-war demonstration in Berkeley, activists came out to DVC to prosecute the case, talking about denial of freedom of speech. I did put my hand up to ask whether they wanted us to defend just free speech or both that and an opposition to the war. The answer was both. The question was pretty naïve, but I was still only 17.

The Vietnam protest movement was growing. The atmosphere everywhere was becoming more political, even in the smaller colleges. I was morally outraged, but it also awoke a political interest. Watching the events on TV, I wanted to know what the answer was, what the demonstrations were about - pro-war, anti-war,

Joel Geier speaking at FSM executive committee meeting, Berkeley, October 1964. Mario Savio seated. Photo: Joel Geier

and freedom of speech. I wasn't radicalised yet, it was rather that I liked newspapers, current affairs and reading about political events.

I started at Berkeley in September 1966, as a second year student. Having come from ultra-suburban Walnut Creek and mild-mannered DVC it was quite an experience. Two issues stood out: Vietnam and civil rights.

My first impression of the campus was much what anyone who starts university feels: "Oh my god, am I up to this? This is the real deal now. It's serious. You've got to work hard if you want to survive." Well, within a year I was saying "Forget about lectures!"

By that time I was interested in politics with a capital P, so I was excited at the idea that there were so many things to do, although my parents' concerns meant I had to be a bit careful. Mostly I hung around the bookstalls.

In 1966 the newly formed Black Panther Party was a new source of inspiration. The Party exploited open-carry gun laws to protect its members when following police cars around in order to record incidents of brutality. This did not endear them to the police and the situation escalated. At one point a notice went up in the German Department saying the Panthers were under attack. The implication seemed to be there was going to be a shootout. I wasn't ready for that, and arranged to be somewhere else.

PUSHING WHEELBARROWS IN YUGOSLAVIA

Arriving for my second visit to Europe in 1967, I was older and ready to ask about socialism. It was time to know about continental Social Democracy, and time to know about the Eastern bloc beyond East Berlin. I travelled around Europe for some weeks before the university year started.

We took the train from London to Paris. Reading my travel diary, I can just picture that time again:

> We came upon three Dutch boys playing guitars, singing and passing the hat. I gave them 20 centimes. Then I got one of the guitars and sang and played "The times they are a-changing". Somebody gave 20 centimes and I was presented with it.

A number of encounters while hitchhiking around Europe had political overtones. I had a long argument (which I enjoyed) with a driver who had lived in Vietnam. He was anti-Gaullist and supported American policies in Vietnam to avoid Chinese domination. I noted down graffiti I saw along the way. "US = Assassins!" "US = 卐". Americans were far from popular in Europe that year:

> Every Italian boy I meet goes: American? Sí? Vietnam? Bang, bang? Have you any idea how I've come to loathe admitting where I'm from?

> When we went back to the hostel we met the expected crowd of Bermuda-clad gringos. We got along fine until they found out my anti-war sentiments. Boy, was that ever a

bang-up argument! They urged me to change my citizenship, the quicker the better.

We met an Italian communist in Florence. Tony told me his ideas:

> About how the Communists will fix the pope's wagon if they ever get into power; about how different the programs must be to run a prosperous country, as opposed to what has been done in Eastern Europe; about how being a Communist didn't keep him from liking Americans.

Then I started to run out of money and it was still weeks before the university year started. Somebody had told me about Yugoslavia's Youth Brigades. So I went to the local authorities in Ljubljana, the capital of Slovenia. From there I made contact with a journalist. We drove down to Zagreb, the capital of Croatia. There I enrolled in a labour brigade (*omladinske nasalje*) where I could have free food and accommodation in return for work.

What on earth was the point of our labour brigade? Certainly not the dam we were ineptly working on.

The Yugoslav state aimed to bring together youth from various backgrounds, mix them all up, put them to work, create a sense of *esprit de corps* and build strong national sentiment and identity in an attempt to overcome divisions between the various republics such as Serbia, Croatia and Bosnia. We can see now, looking back, that it didn't work. But at the time it seemed plausible to me as a still naïve teenager. It was like a summer camp, except we got to push wheelbarrows for hours daily, which was pretty hard physical labour.

We marched up to evening rallies singing a paean to hard work:

Ide na stupa, Neboj se rada
Ivan Mecar, naibolja brigada.

(Going in a column, don't be afraid of hard work
Ivan Mecar, the best brigade.)

I wrote in my diary:

> Each brigade with its own chant. And it's not forced, it's not staged, it's real – and it's thrilling. And when I learned the songs and the chants I screamed along. No wonder Hitler was a success. Nothing like 40 red flags and a thousand throats.

Ivan Mecar, after whom our brigade was named, had been a Communist organiser of labour "shock" brigades under Stalin. And by the simple expedient of working stupidly hard I was awarded a badge with a big red star and the word *Udarnik* (shock worker) at the end of my stay.

Everyone gave blood for the Vietnamese and so did I. In my diary I commented, "My blood type is O. I hope the Viet Cong appreciates it."

On another occasion I made waves by displaying a badge saying "Kill a Commie for Christ". I told them it was meant ironically, but this failed to convince. I was being challenged on political principles and brought down to earth. Was this socialism?

Daily at 4.00 am, a man with an amazingly loud, grating, gravelly voice stood at the head of my bunk bed, shaking the metal frame, and bellowing "*Ustai! Ustai!*" which means "get up!" This went on every day until the young workers began to get sick and the camp administrators backed off.

For days we worked with the wheelbarrow. Then somebody rolled up with some earth-moving equipment, moving a huge amount of dirt, and doing the job in no time. This is when I became doubtful about the whole work brigade project. Later on I became suspicious about similar operations in Cuba and in Nicaragua. They were projects to get young students to ideologically commit to the regimes, and really had nothing to do with the most efficient way to get the work done.

In Croatia I could sometimes get by with Russian, given the family resemblance of Slavic languages. Somebody lent me a textbook, and I picked up a lot of Croatian from talking to people. There were a few odd moments though. I got a funny response from a guy one day when I wanted to say "smoking" but in fact used the word for penis.

Later on, I went into a restaurant in Zagreb, and sat down feeling pretty confident about the language. But I was shocked to discover I couldn't understand a single word on the menu! I realised that in the brigade, food was just placed in front of us, and we just ate it – nobody discussed the names of the dishes. I explained the situation to the waiter. In the end, I just said I wanted "normal food", and got meat and potatoes.

I had some political discussions in the camp.

> I made an effort to play devil's advocate. Whereas in the States I'm outspokenly anti-American Vietnam policies, here I said: "Yes, I'm against American involvement – but Ho Chi Minh is no saint either". That shook them up a little. Once I talked for

Newspaper cutting showing Tom (seated second right) with his work brigade at a mayoral reception in Zagreb, August 1967

about two hours with the former brigade commander and local party official Sasha – in Russian! A little halting, but immensely valuable, above all because the point was brought home to me once again that these people think differently…

The other talk I had was with some Czechs – also in Russian. One was a psychology student, and I asked him about the traditionally hostile Communist attitude towards Freud. He said that this had changed, that Communist psychologists now realised Freud was not the farcical figure the Stalinists had made him out to be – and that Pavlov wasn't god either.

They also taught us naughty songs; the most popular slang term seemed to be *partisani* (making out in the bushes like guerrillas). At the final night farewell party,

> We locked arms, shuffled in a circle and sang obscene songs for hours. I've never heard vulgarity like these kids used at camp.

The party ended, "I kissed 10,000 people on both cheeks", and I headed off to Germany.

Some months later spring vacation made possible a return to the Balkans, travelling to Bulgaria and lodging in people's spare rooms. The host in Sofia was a Communist Party member who spoke French, and defended his government's policies. The USA had better machines, he conceded, but everybody in Bulgaria had a job.

"EVERYONE TALKS ABOUT THE WEATHER – NOT US."

Tom's passport showing multiple short visits to East Berlin

In 1967-68, I spent a year at the University of Göttingen, in the north of what was then West Germany. I went on the exchange program partly to get away from parental control. My initial interest was doing something different, something my parents would be nervous about, but it soon focused into politics.

Germany seemed pretty quiet at first, especially in the small university town of Göttingen. But the first orientation sessions for US exchange students began to change the mood. The purpose of these sessions was mainly to get our German up to scratch, but the orientation rapidly became a forum for discussion because most of the Californian students there were political, that being the nature of the period. We discussed some of the practical obstacles facing the second-rate East German economy. Maybe the GDR had some excuses for its failings?

I straight away became a member of the German SDS (*Sozialistischer Deutscher Studentenbund*, Socialist German Student Union), basically because as soon as I got away from my parents I joined the most radical organisation I could find. Almost immediately I got involved in organising a demonstration against the Vietnam War, drawing the American exchange students into this anti-American demonstration – a very satisfying experience!

There was a slight problem: the SDS burnt the American flag. And I hadn't been consulted about this, so I came under considerable political pressure immediately, from people who were more radical than I was. I went to my first SDS branch meeting, and made a complaint about burning the American flag, along the lines of "it would breed ethnic hostility and fascism". They argued back. I stuck around.

They set up the SDS after their radicalism resulted in expulsion from the youth section of the SPD (*Sozialdemokratische Partei Deutschlands*, Social Democratic Party of Germany). I was more active than a lot of the German members in my local branch. It was my great opportunity to have political experiences, at least locally – I had no experience of the central organisation. Joining SDS in a way sealed me off from more moderate ideas long enough for the radical ones to take root.

In reaction to a coalition between the SPD and the conservatives, the SDS raised a slogan: *Wer hat uns verraten? Sozialdemokraten* (Who betrayed us? The Social Democrats). Another popular slogan was: *Alle Reden vom Wetter – wir nicht!* (Everyone talks about the weather – not us!).

Instead they taught Marxism, albeit a rather confused version. For instance, I had a badge from the Chinese consulate in East Berlin announcing that "A single spark can spark a prairie fire". This was a politics of individual actions, different from the Marxist philosophy of collective struggle. But none of the SDS leaders in Göttingen picked me up on it. In fact, some of the national leaders were themselves under Maoist influence. The Maoist pattern of thought combined collectivism for the masses with voluntarism for elite cadres, of which Mao's protégé Lin Biao was the model. By this time Lin Biao was on his way out, but the *Little Red Book* with its trite summaries of Mao-thought was still in vogue. I owned a copy but I didn't carry it around for instant reference as one acquaintance did.

The Eastern bloc also had a certain influence in SDS, but this was necessarily limited, because for a reality check we had only to cross the Berlin Wall.

I did this in January 1968, and proudly sent my parents a postcard:

(Clockwise from top) postcard from East Berlin, 1967; Göttingen postcard 1967 showing the market place. Tom remembers standing here and having an argument with a blue collar worker; Tom's radical German friend Dieter Lober

Hi – guess where? Just here for a weekend – scrimped and saved to pay for it. This is East Berlin...in the GDR, if you recall the abbreviation. The next socialist card will be from Poland this Spring.

Visiting Berlin this time was very different from my first visit. While at high school in America, there had been a chance to have a pen pal in East Germany. I was amazed that this was allowed by the authorities from either end, but I grabbed at the opportunity and Sophie became my pen pal. I thought, "I'll go there sometime, and I'll have somebody I know to meet, and in the meantime I'll have this opportunity to use the language." I made the correspondence as political as possible, but the trouble was that East Germans saw their politics as tedious and tiresome. However Sophie was interested in me because I was exotic - an American. I did occasionally draw her into political conversations which were very revealing, mostly along the lines of my looking for something good to say about East Germany, which she never did.

Initially Sophie was just someone to exchange letters with. But in that year it was great to have a pen pal in Berlin. Visiting her, as I did periodically, gave me exposure to a genuine East German family environment. I dragged Sophie into political discussions because this was an opportunity. I thought, "Politics in East Germany, for god's sake: how could anyone not want to do this?!"

By now Sophie had become more political. Then I got to know her parents. Her father had been in prison for trying to cross the Wall. I made facile arguments, and they made obvious ones. To my insistence that Western capitalism had its own evils, he replied: "Maybe we don't want capitalism, but we sure don't want Communism." To my arguments about things like how badly made American cars were and planned obsolescence, Sophie answered tellingly: "I doubt if I'll ever own an American car."

Sophie didn't want to spend all afternoon in her parents' place, so we were out and about, which gave me the opportunity to observe East German life. Once in a lift there was a conversation going on. The woman said "We have to do something to help the state," and the man looked at her and said "It's necessary!" The state was a disaster and needed all the help it could get. I just grinned and they grinned back.

This helped counter my fanciful

48 "Everyone talks about the weather – not us."

idea of what socialism should be like. Talking to people who actually lived in the East made it clear to me that real socialism was not merely state planning and the authority of the state. It had to be a liberation, a step into freedom.

Our interaction was not without repercussions for Sophie. One day she was approached on campus by a complete stranger who said "You're writing to an American." He wanted to show that they knew. That was how the Stasi operated.

A team of politically hardened GDR academics visited Göttingen. They got sharp criticism from the SDS members, who wanted to know why citizens of a (supposedly) liberated state couldn't travel abroad. That evening in a public meeting they got even more of a thrashing:

Audience: Over there you rig the votes.
The speaker: Not true. Take the recent referendum. Do you know what the yes vote was?
The crowd, jeering: 99 percent!
The speaker: A typical case of *denkste* (think-so) – It was 94 percent!
Laughter from the crowd.

Some weeks later I was back in East Berlin and saw the same speaker coming out of a bookshop full of GDR propaganda, which few local citizens would go near. He was wearing elegant Western sandals of the sort few local citizens would ever get to wear. A reminder of Sophie and the American cars.

One interesting thing about the relationship between East and West Germany was the common language. Each side had linguistic access to material from the other side. This was exploited by both regimes. There was an electronic billboard relating the latest news across the top of a building on the West Berlin side, right at the border crossing. It was weird to read this from the East Berlin side, where it was clearly visible.

On the other side there was an East German propaganda TV channel called *Der Schwarze Kanal* (the Black Channel) whose role was to debunk the West German media. Only hard-line East German supporters would watch it. Most East Germans watched West German TV – that was the source of information. I remember Sophie's father saying, "I haven't watched any TV lately, I don't know the latest news." – meaning that newspapers were no use at all. I would always read the newspapers because I wanted to get a feel for things, but they seldom provided that.

"More and more red flags!"

Rudi Dutschke, SDS national leader and the most prominent spokesperson of the German radical student movement, gave a speech in Göttingen in April 1968. Members of the campus community, previously hostile, queued for tickets. He was a good speaker and in his prime, not charismatic but really solid, a lot of emphasis on substance. Nobody could have predicted that three weeks later he would be lying in intensive care after being shot in the head by a young anti-communist.

The student movement blamed this assassination attempt on the tabloids of the Springer press (equivalent to Murdoch). They had been agitating among the populace against us students, trying to create hysteria, calling us long-haired apes and so on. So we set out to shut down the Springer press. Although this was totally too ambitious, the students tried and in the larger cities like Hamburg, Frankfurt, Munich and Berlin they used tactics we still use – linking arms, trying to stop the trucks, like a picket line.

But even nationally we didn't have the forces, and we certainly didn't have the forces in Göttingen. We had only about 50-70 people when we issued a call to blockade the mail trucks and the *Bild-Zeitung* (a scurrilous tabloid similar to the British *Sun*) came out as scheduled.

We then turned our attention to how the newspapers were transported to Göttingen and we received the information – which turned out to be false – that they came by post. So we decided that to stop the Springer press we had to stop the mail! This

Auditorium of Göttingen university from 1967 postcard

posed the problem that the legislated punishment for disrupting the post is pretty severe. We turned up at the delivery point in large numbers, which shrank as sections of the crowd kept slinking away to the nearest bar.

Ultimately we were not allowed to *see* the mail – that would have been a dereliction of duty on the part of the postal authorities – but we were allowed to stick our hands into the postal bags and *feel* in there – no newspapers. By now it was midnight. We got up the next morning to see the papers which were on sale in all the kiosks, and of course they were all about Frankfurt, Hamburg and so on. So in the end we didn't really accomplish much.

There was an interesting spin-off from all this. In the aftermath of Rudi Dutschke being shot, the East German radio broadcast a description from a demonstration in West Berlin. This was a golden opportunity for the East German government. The journalist got very excited watching this demo, and kept yelling out "*Rote Fahnen! immer mehr rote Fahnen!*" (red flags, more and more red flags!), "oh my god, there are red flags everywhere."

The change in the East German attitude to the student demonstrations had a funny consequence for me personally. Some weeks previously I had been frisked at the crossing point into East Berlin. The East Berlin border guards staged a scary, bullying interrogation – "Go into that little room, you. Why do you speak German? Take your shoes off, shake them, see if there's anything in those shoes." The guards wanted to know who was this guy, he's an American, why is he coming here all the time? They were quite aggressive, they didn't like me.

Crossing again after the demonstrations, I had my Karl Marx badge ready, although it had never done me any good. This time, I went to the checkpoint at Friedrichstrasse, passed the West German authorities who were none too friendly, to be welcomed enthusiastically into East Berlin: "*Guten Morgen, Herr Linkoln*". It was quite striking, their whole attitude had turned around because of the demonstration. They must have been under instructions to make the crossing a welcoming line into East Berlin.

A rousing rendition of the Internationale

In February 1968 I had visited Paris and saw the first round of student actions of that famous year. I had been used to bland anti-war demonstrations where we sang "Give Peace a Chance". Here were some 20,000 students and leftists with deadly serious looks, demanding victory. In his remarkable book *The Fire Last Time*, Chris Harman says that French radical movements were smaller in February than elsewhere in Europe. This was not my observation. But either way, what was clear at the time was the growing power of these movements.

So, during that spring, we students in Germany were aware that there was a huge fight brewing in France. In early May, Daniel Cohn-Bendit, who was a leader of the French student movement, visited Germany and afterwards had difficulty returning to France. The newspapers reported that he was stuck on the German side of the border. We had a teach-in going in Göttingen, when late in the day, a young man got up and made an announcement: "Daniel Cohn-Bendit has arrived in Paris!" A great cheer went up and everyone stood and started singing *La Marseillaise*: "*Allons enfants de la patrie...*" But the guy got up again and said, "Comrades, no no no no no, *La Marseillaise* is a bourgeois anthem!" So we all sang a rousing rendition of the *Internationale*!

At the end of the university year, I again travelled around Europe. It was the summer of 1968, and there seemed to be much to hope for as the train left Berlin in June for

Prague. Perhaps even "socialism with a human face". The future was very unclear, but a man in a Prague café raised his beer mug and said to me in uncertain German, "*Ich bin Freiling*": he was free.

I didn't know it, but in faraway Australia, the Communist Party was also delighted with the events in Czechoslovakia. A correspondent from Prague wrote to their newspaper *Tribune*:

> This country has taken an enormous step forward – and I am so glad… Here we stand on firm ground to beat the whole concept of "Western way of life" in its entire ramifications. This is the "cultural revolution" which is utterly and completely invincible! There will be no H.G. Wells society; there will be, however, a free cultured, dignified mankind much more wonderful than William Morris dared to dream.[9]

Coming back to Paris in August I stayed in a youth hostel in the 19th arrondissement, which was run by a bunch of anarchists. It was there I met Janey Stone. While we were there, the Russians invaded Czechoslovakia, putting an end to that hope generated by the Prague Spring, and teaching us all something about the nature of the so-called communist societies.

I had by this time a year of political activism under my belt. Allowing for naivety and inexperience, you could say I was a Marxist. After Rudi Dutschke was shot and what were effectively riots outside the Springer press, I was hardened up; I had crossed a boundary in attitude.

I had not yet read much Marx, just a few of the basic things, like the *Communist Manifesto*. I was more likely to read Lenin on imperialism. For me at that time, it wasn't that clear what the *Manifesto* was for, it was too long ago, whereas Lenin had died only 40 years earlier, only a generation or two away. We celebrated the Russian Revolution as something relatively recent. And that celebration was organised not by Marxists but just by people who wanted to celebrate it. Thus Lenin seemed much more real to us than Marx, Lenin was perceived as connected to action, whereas Marx was considered more theoretical. There was no specific individual person who influenced me more than others. I listened to the things that were being said around me and would go and read about them.

I took this interest in listening to political argument and ideas back with me to Berkeley.

"I ONLY SEE YOU AT REVOLUTIONS"

I returned in August 1968 to a very different United States, marked by riots, incipient rebellion and political fallout mounting from the Vietnamese Tet Offensive. It was time to confront American liberalism with the Marxist analysis learned in Göttingen, but for me with a reservation: that a new philosophical framework must make revolution inseparable from democracy. Just such an approach offered itself in the Independent Socialists (soon to be renamed the International Socialists).

The SDS had taught me Marxism. Now here I was planning to teach all the Berkeley radicals about it, but they were way ahead of me. They had read Lenin, even Trotsky, and the Independent Socialists were putting out the most original writings.

This group, whose best known leader was Hal Draper, made a splash during the FSM. For me, they opened the door to a new political tradition: "Shachtmanism", associated with one of Trotsky's most important collaborators in the US, Max Shachtman. From here the next step was the ideas of Tony Cliff, who led a promising left group in Britain.

After Shachtman abandoned revolutionary politics in the 1950s, Draper had become the key leader of the group, producing an influential pamphlet called *The Two Souls of Socialism*, and coining the term "socialism from below". A crotchety fellow, Draper had a firm sense of his own rightness, which carried him through those difficult years: better than ambiguity to my mind.

I was already interested in socialism, which I had thought I would

Tom in Northside Berkeley, 1970s

find in Europe. But neither social democracy, such as in France or Scandinavia, nor East Germany was what I wanted.

So my search led me to talking to all the people on the bookstalls on the Berkeley campus. I also argued with Hubert the Evangelist, who stood on the steps at Bancroft Avenue with his Bible and lectured us on sin. Going to argue with him and going to argue with the reds, the left - I was happy to argue with any of them on any given day. For a time it was just an intellectual thing, it was what you were at university for, to educate yourself, challenge your ideas: "Look at me, I can even argue about religion! And communism!"

But really I was looking for something that would give me a political framework. So after some time it became a routine thing to talk to the different left groups.

I found the Socialist Workers Party boring and conservative. They would lecture young activists with phrases like "Don't you know that's illegal?" Reading their publications was intellectually useful, but I found them socially conservative. They even used to wear ties.

American Students for a Democratic Society (SDS) lacked a sizeable branch in Berkeley, but there was still a very large broad left milieu of independent radical activists who were proudly the "New Left". They wanted to bring trouble to the bosses, the ruling class. There was a sense of great excitement and something new happening.

At the same time there were some things about Maoism that appealed to me. I was attracted initially by the idea of the Third World struggle. I remember Tom Hayden saying "A new International is opening up, the Vietnamese, the Palestinians, and so

Pages from Tom's 1967 Berkeley scrapbook

on". In this atmosphere, as a white revolutionary, you were looking for some force that could challenge the system. Che Guevara's appeal was also very similar to that of the Maoists. It was the same phenomenon, of looking for a Third World champion.

As to the Communist Party, they were talking about a mass party, which at the time just seemed to be too hard. The CP however thought in terms of an army. This contrasted with Guevarists who thought in terms of the heroics of a small band of revolutionaries. We tended to regard the CP members with contempt. The famous phrase "Never trust anybody over 30" was uttered by Jack Weinberg (an IS member) in response to a journalist asking "What about the Communist Party?" It was conventional to think of them as just a bunch of old fogeys.

However, my own reaction when I finally actually encountered the CP in person was different. The term "communist" had been used successfully during the Cold War as a term of fear. And then I actually saw some Communists at a bookstall with some of their literature. I had read some of their material, but I'd never actually seen it on a table in a public place. It felt very strange.

In April 1969, students occupied a waste site owned by the university and used as a carpark, and began to turn it into a park which was also intended to be an off-campus space for free speech, rallies and political organisation.

People's Park lasted for three weeks. The hippies wanted to turn a dirt car park into the Garden of Eden, but the university insisted on its property rights. That's capitalism. But did the cops really have to open up on demonstrators with shotguns? To stop a hippie park? They used buckshot; and a demonstrator died. Eventually Ronald Reagan, governor of California, declared martial law, sent in the National Guard, and we had a situation where you couldn't go out at night without specific permission.

Did Reagan really have to declare martial law? It only lent credibility to the *San Francisco Chronicle* when they published Adolf Hitler's notorious "we need law and order" speech and linked it with Reagan.

In the aftermath there were illegal demonstrations. If you've seen the film *Berkeley in the Sixties*, you'll have seen the cops suppressing an illegal assembly using a helicopter belching tear gas. We watched the helicopter from a second storey balcony of Dwinelle Hall on the campus. On another day, I watched from the same

Kathleen Cleaver

Cathleen and Eldridge Cleaver were leaders of the Black Panthers

Eldridge Cleaver 1968

WHO OWNS THE PARK?

Someday a petty official will appear with a piece of paper, called a land title, which states that the University of California owns the land of the People's Park. Where did that piece of paper come from? What is it worth?

A long time ago the Costanoan Indians lived in the area now called Berkeley. They had no concept of land ownership. They believed that the land was under the care and guardianship of the people who used it and lived on it.

Catholic missionaries took the land away from the Indians. No agreements were made. No papers were signed. They ripped it off in the name of God.

The Mexican Government took the land away from the Church. The Mexican Government had guns and an army. God's word was not as strong.

The Mexican Government wanted to pretend that it was not the army that guaranteed them the land. They drew up some papers which said they legally owned it. No Indians signed those papers.

The Americans were not fooled by the papers. They had a stronger army than the Mexicans. They beat them in a war and took the land. Then they wrote some papers of their own and forced the Mexicans to sign them.

The American Government sold the land to some white settlers. The Government gave the settlers a piece of paper called a land title in exchange for some money. All this time there were still some Indians around who claimed the land. The American army killed most of them.

The piece of paper saying who owned the land was passed around among rich white men. Sometimes the white men were interested in taking care of the land. Usually they were just interested in making money. Finally some very rich men, who run the University of California, bought the land.

Immediately these men destroyed the houses that had been built on the land. The land went the way of so much other land in America—it became a parking lot.

We are building a park on the land. We will take care of it and guard it, in the spirit of the Costanoan Indians. When the University comes with its land title we will tell them: "Your land title is covered with blood. We won't touch it. Your people ripped off the land from the Indians a long time ago. If you want it back now, you will have to fight for it again."

The university owned a vacant lot. Hippies turned it into a park! The university insisted on its property rights

All photos on p 2, 3 by Grossman

spot as my brother Terry, with his shirt off, led a phalanx of rock-throwing students whose charge drove the cops back. That was awesome, in the original sense of the word.

My most daring foray was joining an illegal march west of the campus, right past the place where the Grateful Dead had played in 1968. The National Guard, looking like the cast from *MASH*, surrounded us, bayonets and all. Having taken my Viet Cong badge off and got out of sight, I was able to escape into a department store and then step out of a side entrance. Looked right, looked left…and there was a row of National Guards with fixed bayonets, marching straight down the alley. I thought it was obvious I was a demonstrator trying to get away from the cops. But I flattened myself against the wall and as they marched past, one of them looked at me and winked as if to say "We're on your side." In fact, many *were* on our side. One of them threw down his gun on national television as a protest.

They arrested 400 demonstrators the day of that march in West Berkeley, and treated them pretty badly. That was a big mistake, because they accidentally grabbed a reporter, who then published the whole scandal.

This was my first experience of an illegal activity. A peaceful, legal march followed on Sunday. It was far bigger, but the impact was smaller.

People's Park was very important. The left has a tendency to treat it as a second-class event, not very significant, a bunch of hippies. There certainly were hippies involved in the construction of the park. But the political consequences went well beyond that. Although all the hippies did was to turn up the soil and plant plants, in doing that they were threatening the police powers of the state, challenging the right of the university to control its property.

When I think of Berkeley as a place, I think of a number of layers – you could see the class pattern pretty clearly in the geography. You started with the treed area of the Berkeley Hills, where the upper middle classes lived. Then there was a sloping area down towards the bay. As you moved down, you went through some very nice houses and also university property such as tennis courts. Then you came down to the campus area and reached a flat geographical formation going down to the bay.

The main counter-culture area was Telegraph Avenue on Southside, a stretch of four blocks, with records, music, books, cafes, and, unofficially, drugs. A hippie centre. West of that, past the business street Shattuck

Avenue, you started getting to the Black area, which was run down, with a lot of boarded-up windows and the like, and it ceased to have much to do with the campus.

When many people hear "Berkeley" they think students and hippies. And that is also part of it for me. The memories are still there: the Doors playing at the Fillmore Ballroom. And a young band playing for free on the sidewalk west of the campus. Their name? Grateful Dead.

I was in Berkeley a few years ago and the radical atmosphere has gone. There is little countercultural presence in Telegraph Avenue today. No sex, drugs and rock and roll!

In the late 1960s, there really was a feeling around that anything was possible. Although in fact I got frightened easily and wasn't very good at fighting the police, and tended to watch from a safe distance, the atmosphere was contagious, it was part of the landscape. Radicalism was the norm: I clearly remember the call of a demonstrator behind me one day: "Hey, I only see you at revolutions!"

This atmosphere intensified in my last two years at Berkeley. The Tet Offensive in 1968 had signalled the failure of American policy in Vietnam. But by a cruel irony, this only opened the way for Richard Nixon to widen the scope of the conflict. In 1970, he authorised the invasion of Cambodia. Extending the war to Cambodia was Nixon's worst crime, far worse than anything he did to cover up Watergate.

There was an enormous wave of protests throughout the country, reaching a climax when students were killed at Kent State, Ohio and Augusta, Georgia. While students were on strike elsewhere, activities at Berkeley centred around the somewhat utopian demand to "reconstitute the university". This could be pretty pointless. Jack Bloom from the IS told one rally about a poetry class that, being poetry, was declared "automatically reconstituted".

At its best, on the other hand, this demand could have had a radical edge. The movement's delegate to the German Department, where I was, dared to put it bluntly: we wanted an automatic pass in every graduate class, leaving us time to agitate all day long. The administration representative took a deep breath… and conceded the demand, leaving us to contemplate what mad effrontery we had pulled off. I submitted an essay on Marxism and Literature; we cut all classes, did no course work, and passed.

I had spent the academic year

Berkeley Under Guard

National Guardsmen wielding bayoneted rifles protected UC's statewide offices at Center and Fulton streets

martial law declared

PIGS SHOOT TO KILL-- BYSTANDERS GUNNED DOWN

Berkeley Barb

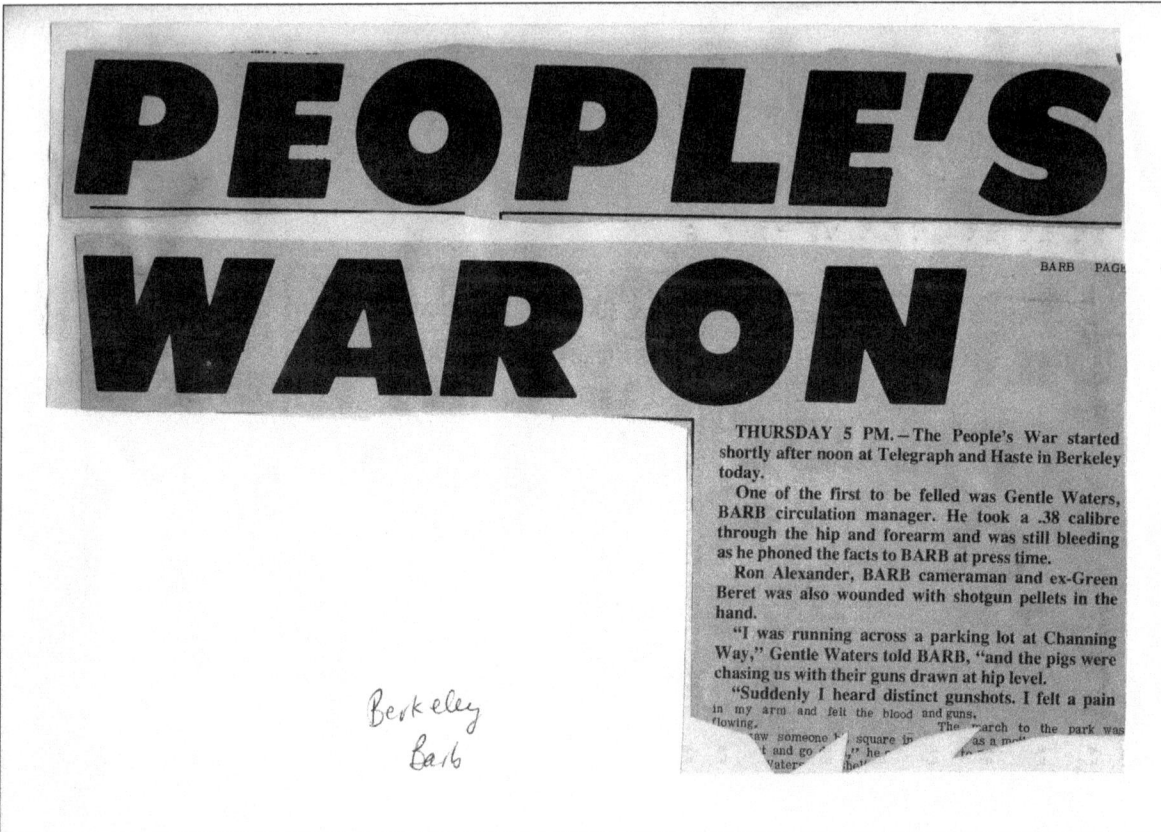

1968-69 sampling the political smorgasbord on offer in Berkeley. But then came the crucial turning point when I finally felt the need to join an organisation.

After Janey arrived we joined the International Socialists in October 1969. In the following two years until we left the US to go to Australia, the IS gave us a political grounding and unforgettable experiences.

Having selected the IS, I thought I knew all about it. But then I spent a week reading all the stuff from the organisation I'd just joined and I was amazed at how many insights there were. I couldn't stop reading. The fact that the IS was out there in a world of theoretical and practical intervention, that was fighting for a certain set of ideas, was a major influence in determining where I ended up.

I was a graduate student in those two years, and Janey worked at a hospital in San Francisco, commuting across the Bay Bridge every day. We went to endless meetings, joined in demonstrations and picket lines, organised and argued. Everything was new. We lived a student lifestyle not dissimilar to that of students today.

Except – it was in Berkeley.

BERSERKELEY!

In March 2016 we recorded a conversation between Joel Geier (one of the leaders of the Berkeley IS at the time we were members), Janey Stone, Robert Zocchi and me.

Joel: I arrived in Berkeley in 1963. I had been in the Young People's Socialist League (YPSL). I had been a leader. I participated in an intense faction fight involving Max Shachtman over entry into the Democratic Party and therefore a movement to the right politically and it really had destroyed the YPSL. So I decided I wanted to go to graduate school, and I wanted to do that in a "quiet" place, somewhere where there wouldn't be too much activity. I picked Berkeley [laughter]. I was also attracted to Hal Draper, who was there. Also, at Berkeley I could sign up in history, the history of the socialist and communist movement in Germany, Russia and France. You could do that in Berkeley in the 60s!

There wasn't yet a branch of the IS as we were still in the YPSL and Socialist Party. In 1962 YPSL probably had 1,000 members, but by 1964 the faction fight had destroyed it and there were far fewer members. So we were members of YPSL but in September 1963 we set up a group called Campus CORE (Congress of Racial Equality) which was the largest group on campus. It mobilised students for the sit-ins in San Francisco and other places and became an important factor in the civil rights movement in the Bay Area. The Free Speech Movement actually started because the authorities were trying to suppress student involvement in the civil rights movement.

Above: newsletter of Berkeley I.S., January 1970

The Berkeley Independent Socialist Club was formed on 13 September 1964, same night as the Free Speech Movement. In fact, we moved the starting time of our meeting from 7.30 to 6.00 so that people could leave the meeting to go to the meeting that formed the FSM. Mario Savio and Jack Weinberg were both at our initial meeting and left from there to go to the formation meeting.

Then five years later, on Labor Day in September of 1969, the ISCs merged with some split offs from SDS and became a national organisation and was renamed the International Socialists.

Tom: I find people just associate Berkeley and the FSM and assume I was there, for example the Marxism 2016 program has a picture of the FSM against my name. I was actually still a high school student then, in Germany! I didn't see the famous speech except later in a video. But I do remember seeing Mario Savio selling books in the prominent Moe's Books.

Janey and I joined the IS in October 1969, which was very soon after its formation. By then I had hung around bookstalls and talked to many different groups. So what made me decide on the IS? Well, you wouldn't be joining the IS if you wanted to lead a revolution immediately – the group was too small. For that you needed an army. What I did find in the IS was a sophisticated line. I could have sophisticated arguments with all these other people by being in the IS. I admired their fluency and

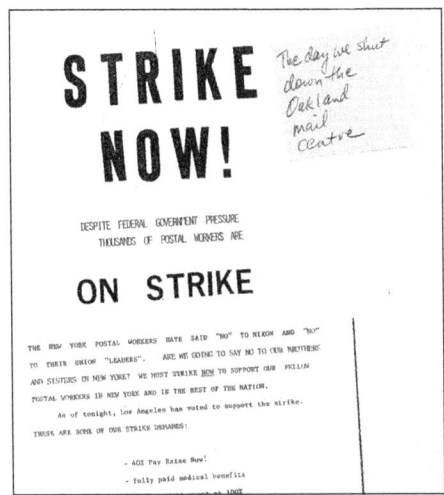

their knowledge. At a recent Socialist Alternative event, a younger member said she liked my intervention because of its fluency and knowledge. Well that's exactly how I felt about the people I heard when I first joined the IS. I wanted to be like them.

On a different level, another thing that attracted me to the IS was their sense of humour, use of cartoons and so on.

Joel: I think the fact that we had a sense of humour meant that we were human beings, as opposed to some of the more uptight leftists who did not know how to relate to other people.

Janey: But it wasn't all humorous. When I think back, I picture a branch meeting with 30 or 40 or 50 people sitting around the office we rented on Telegraph Avenue. I remember meetings strictly starting on time. If you were late, you'd miss that part of the meeting. The discussions were conducted with five minute rounds, that is, each person could speak for up to five minutes. Then you'd have a second round. The call list was as long as your arm, as everybody had lots to say. And the meetings would go until 11 or 11.30 or even later.

Joel: It was the university rule we used: you start ten minutes after the hour, period. The attitude was, if you can get there for your class, you can get there for the meeting. These long meetings were the remnants of the Trotskyist movement.

There were some really heated meetings in 1966 that went on way past midnight. Discussing things like whether we should accept the military draft or not. This was actually a very important issue at the time. The tradition of the Trotskyist movement was derived from the Bolsheviks. You would serve in the army, learn how to use guns, when the revolution breaks out you know who to use them against. Also, we ask for no special privileges, the working class goes in so we go in.

But then we were confronted with

Flyer for picket at Oakland Mail Centre, 1970 postal strike; *Oakland Tribune*, 1970; (opposite page) Promo for Tom's first talk related to Marxism in the Berkeley I.S. newsletter, January 1970. Cartoon by Lisa Lyons. This was a take off of a well known Peanuts cartoon of Snoopy writing his novels

Berserkeley!

the draft resistance movement, and should we support it? It was a part of the anti-war movement, after all. All these meetings went on past midnight and it was the older comrades from World War II who all had very strong points of view on it. Some said you should go into it. Others said "and so-and-so was killed, and so-and-so was killed". In the end we came out in support of the draft resisters. Years later we thought we probably made a mistake because of the enormous resistance that existed inside the American army, the revolt of the troops and so on. During World War II, there was no resistance in the American army. There was some at the end of the war, in the Philippines, the Bring the Boys Home movement and all that. But in the Vietnam War, after the Tet offensive, there was a fantastic resistance in the army, the army collapsed.

Janey: Even though I was working, I was in the campus branch with Tom. We still had a student mentality. But I do remember members who were workers saying how ridiculous it was to have these meetings going on past midnight when they had to work the next day. I seem to remember a bit of tension between the campus branch and the community branch. The workers in the community branch, with justification, thought they were more grown up given they were workers and older.

Joel: We also had university workers as members. They were in the clerical workers' union. In 1966 there was a student strike against military recruitment on campus, and two secretaries, both of them members of the IS, walked off the job, saying "Workers on campus are also against the war and have something to say about it." They organised for campus workers to walk off in support of the student strike. And from that they started to organise the union, with older comrades giving them advice on how to build the union from the ground up, setting up shop committees and things like that. Then the Communist Party came along and co-operated with us and so on.

Tom: There were enormous anti-war demonstrations at the time, perhaps the biggest I have ever been in. There were two national demonstrations, one in Washington and one in San Francisco. I remember Leonard Nimoy – *Start Trek's* Mr Spock – speaking at one of these, at one of the large football stadiums in San Francisco. He was quite serious about the anti-war stance. Those demos had to have a very long route because when the first people were arriving at the destination, some people still hadn't left the start. It was an all-day thing!

Joel: They used to hold these demonstrations approximately twice a year. One would be East Coast, either New York or Washington, the other West Coast, either San Francisco or Los Angeles. They were big. They grew to anything from half a million to two million people, and the biggest ones were between 1969 and 1971. The demos were dominated by the Communist Party and the Socialist Workers Party. There was all sorts of political infighting over the character of the demonstration. The two parties had competing coalitions which each tried to organise their own event. Finally, at the end, they'd be forced to co-operate and have a joint demonstration.

The CP and the SWP were involved in the organisation, but the thing is that no matter who called them and no matter what the official slogans were, the population was against the war; they would just pour out. The CP's coalition would be for "negotiations now" and various other demands. The SWP's coalition would be for "immediate withdrawal". "Bring the troops home now" was their slogan. They would raise nothing else – nothing about racism or the wage freeze or anything like that. These two groups would fight over who the speakers would be and so on, but 99 percent of the people there would be totally unaware of all this, or couldn't care less, they were just there to oppose the war.

Now these big demos were twice a year. But throughout the rest of the year there was constantly stuff happening on the ground. For me, the best demonstration in the Bay Area was the Stop the Draft week, September 1967, in which we shut down downtown Oakland, barricaded it, tried to prevent the Draft Board from functioning – it was the most radical of the demonstrations.

I think Berkeley was the centre of the world radical movement for some years! The world identified with Berkeley. I remember getting on a train in Europe in 1968, talking to someone, we had no language in common. He said to me something like "Americano?", I said "Berkeley", and then he went "Ahhh, radicale!" I said "No! Revoluzionaire!!"

Tom: The IS industrial work was an important part of my political education. I remember a postal strike which started out as a mass strike on the East Coast, then rolled westward and lost momentum. By the time it got to California, it was not going to be able to match the struggles in the East, it was floundering. Nonetheless, we went down to the Oakland mail centre and put up a picket line. Then all these people turned up and said "Oh, picket line, better go home." They wanted to go on strike but they had no leadership. In effect, we, as outsiders, set up a picket line and workers responded. That was the atmosphere. They wanted someone to set up a picket line.

Then there was the teamsters. There was a wave of unrest in the Teamsters' union and we tried to plug into that. The teamsters in LA held a wildcat strike. They wanted to spread the strike to the Bay Area and they sent the biggest guys I'd ever seen, gigantic guys, to set up pickets to convince teamsters in the Bay Area to come out on strike. My involvement with the teamsters came down to attending one picket line. You went out there and you were out there until three in the morning or something. It left a big impression on me and I still remember it well. I was amazed at how big and strong these guys were and I tried to fit in by saying "fuck" a lot.

Joel: Our comrades in the Los Angeles IS group, whose names you'd know, Bob Brenner, Sam Farber and others, had a group called Picket Line. They came down to the picket line and became involved with these teamsters, started writing leaflets for them, became closely aligned with them. So when the teamsters wanted to spread their struggle to the Bay Area, they sent our IS comrades up to help organise and they came to visit our office in Berkeley.

But you have to understand, this was all in the midst of the Cambodia student strike! We were meeting there twice a day during the strike, 7.00 am and 5.30pm. They were our most efficient meetings, lasting one hour. You had to know everything that was going on and exactly what you were going to do. You'd go to work or to your classes, then come to the meeting at 5.30, and it would be over at 6.30 so everyone could go to all the other meetings they needed to get to in order to participate in and link with the various other campaigns.

Well, teamsters would come to our office. Amidst all this, the wildcat teamsters used our office as their organising centre. And they were sleeping there! We also collaborated with the Local and put out a newspaper with them, called *The Fifth Wheel*.

Women's liberation and gay liberation

Janey: One of the most durable memories I have of the Berkeley IS at that time was the strong adoption of women's liberation. I think I caught the crest of the wave there. The IS was one of the first left organisations to respond to the women's liberation movement, which was still pretty small at that time, and not very working class-oriented, unlike in Australia. So many male leaders of left organisations at the time felt threatened, but I don't think that was the case in the IS. Maybe not absolutely everyone was OK with it – there may have been the odd man who felt a bit uncertain. But the atmosphere, which I remember really well, was such that when we had a women's caucus you hardly had any men getting anxious about what women were talking about in a room without men. You kept hearing and reading about the level of paranoia in many of the other organisations. Why was the IS so quick to take ideas of women's liberation on board?

Joel: That was also true in terms of the gay movement. I think there are two things. One: our politics were against all oppression. No shilly-shallying or excuses. You're against oppression. The question comes up and you may not be very sophisticated in the theoretical explanations. But people are raising a question of oppression. Well, we're against it and that's that. Two: there were the traditions of the Trotskyist and Communist movements. People like Anne Draper who had been trained in those politics decades before considered themselves to be women's liberationists. They were the main reasons. Furthermore,

there was just no excuse to be against it. There was also nothing to hold us back. We didn't have to say stuff like "they don't have women's liberation in Russia".

The atmosphere among the women comrades was "thank god it's finally happening". I can't remember any man saying anything like "Well what are they talking about? Are they talking about us?"

Janey: It all came out of the assumption that the women should do the typing, serious decisions are made by men in networks that exclude women, that sort of thing. I think that came out of the SDS. In the Berkeley IS, we had women leaders, political leaders, long before that movement began, and there were a lot of them. Also the women's caucuses were not organised by women who were afraid to speak up. They were people who could speak at mass meetings.

The thing was, though, because of the way the movement operated at the time, it seemed to end up with women having to do everything twice. What I mean is that whatever you discussed in the women's caucus still had to be discussed in the branch anyway. And on top of that we had a women's liberation fraction, that is, those of us who were involved in the broader women's movement had to caucus in preparation for our interventions there. We seemed to have at least twice as many meetings as everyone else!

Having been liberated from the need to straighten her hair, Janey with a Jewish Afro hairstyle, 1973

There were women members who were politically and theoretically developed but we also had women members who weren't, who had suffered from the effects of women's oppression, who didn't speak out. The women's caucuses attempted to develop that ability to speak out. The women's caucus was certainly valuable to me because at the time I didn't talk much in meetings – you won't remember me getting up and giving five-minute speeches!

Robert: I'm really impressed with the early response of the IS to gay and lesbian liberation. Because in the case of women, at least there was a long history of women's political involvement in, for example, the Communist Parties. But there was not the same kind of tradition in these parties on the question of homosexuality. And yet the IS was able to immediately say, when the question arose in a big public way, "yep, we're against the oppression of gays and lesbians". Joel, do you remember some of the early responses to the appearance of the Gay Liberation Front?

Joel: Well, I can go back to when I joined in the organisation in 1960. We had prominent gay leaders. Bayard Rustin, the organiser of the March on Washington, the enormous Black demonstration in 1963, probably the most prominent and publicly gay person in the country, was a member. And we had long had a general atmosphere of sexual liberation. In the 50s, under McCarthyism! And that had to include same-sex attraction. I remember, as a new and very young member, when I made a remark about a leading male member who slept with one of the younger male comrades, the established members came down on me like a ton of bricks, saying "gay people are entitled to choose their sex partners like anyone else is". This is years before the Gay Liberation Front.

All this really goes back to the Communist movement in the 1920s, the Young Communist League of the time, that sort of thing. Now we didn't have a very sophisticated theoretical view about gay liberation. And it should be said that Rustin, for such a public gay, didn't want to make that a political question. Martin Luther King would not defend him on this question. But in our milieu, sexuality was all public. We didn't think it was the most important political question to fight on at the time, but we thought there was nothing wrong with being gay, so when the Gay Liberation came, our attitude was: it's about fuckin' time!

Tom: I remember distinctly that there were protests against the SWP, who were slow on the uptake, and I remember people organising a picket of their national conference in around 1969. The reason this sticks in my mind is that in 1973, George Novack, a leader of the SWP, came out to Australia on a speaking tour and had the effrontery to suggest, in front of a large audience, that the SWP was well in advance of the rest of the American left on the question of gay liberation.

Joel: He wished! The SWP *expelled* gay members well into the 1970s. Partly this was because they were pro-Castro, and at that point in time, gays in Cuba were locked up. If you had a different position, how would you justify it? The SWP tried to justify everything the Cuban government was doing. They also made arguments like "workers won't like it" and "the FBI will be able to lean on you" – all sorts of crap like that.

The difficulty they had was that the radical movement was moving in a pro-gay direction. Not everyone – for example, the Maoists were against gays, although there were Maoists who were gay and in the closet. But generally, the broad left was pro-gay. So some SWP members started to complain: "Why is our group behind the rest of the left? Why are we taking reactionary positions?" So more and more of their members came out. And they finally had to do a flip-flop. I don't remember the exact year, but there was a big fight about this. The explanation for Novack's behaviour that you described, Tom, was that he just didn't want to say anything embarrassing about his group.

Robert: You seem to be saying that at first they put forward forceful political arguments as to why they were expelling gays while other groups were more along the lines of umming and aahing and not really knowing what to do. In fact, if I'm not wrong, the British IS also ummed and aahed on this question at first.

Joel: Cliff once said to me, referring to our American newspaper, "*Workers Power* is a sex magazine", because there were all these articles about women's liberation and gay liberation. And I said to him, "Just wait till it gets to Britain! You don't know what you're in for!" Barry Sheppard wrote a book about the history of the SWP in which he talks about this.[10]

A pre-revolutionary period?

Janey: The atmosphere at Berkeley in the two years I was there, 1969 to 1971, I will never forget. There were hippies, lefties, students, then a series of workers' disputes. There was a certain atmosphere at that time. I remember being at a small women's liberation meeting in someone's living room, and somebody said, "Now that we've had the revolution, what happens next?" People were using the word "revolution" rather loosely, but there was that sense of change, wasn't there? I remember Joel saying in a branch meeting, "we're not in a revolutionary period, and we're not in a pre-revolutionary period, but we are in the period before that". In retrospect, that was somewhat too hopeful!

Joel: Our general attitude was that it was a pre-revolutionary period in the "weak links" – France, Italy, Spain, Portugal and Greece, also in Argentina, Chile and Uruguay – and there was a radicalisation in other places that was not pre-revolutionary. We thought that if some of those weak links snapped, then it would spread. That was our attitude up to about the defeat of the Portuguese Revolution in late 1975. Maybe even for a year after that, because of the hope that it might spread to Spain. The radical upsurge began in 1968 in Paris. And remember there were half a million people in the US who considered themselves to be revolutionaries, what with the wildcat strikes in the teamsters – certainly hundreds of thousands of people. We did not go overboard to say that it was a pre-revolutionary situation. Revolution was on the agenda. Not in the US, but elsewhere.

You can see how we felt when you think about how just recently, in Tunisia and Egypt, we all started to feel that revolution was on the agenda again. Of course, that shut down a lot more quickly than the period from 1968 to 1975. But while it's happening there is a feeling of endless possibilities.

Tom: I remember that we used to cooperate at times with the Communist Party. At one point Anne Draper was planning a cavalcade to go down to the California Central Valley to support the farmworkers. But before that happened, there was some event the previous day which must have seen some bitter factional differences between us and the CP. And the forces seemed roughly balanced, this being Berkeley and not Detroit.

Joel: There certainly were plenty of times when we collaborated with the CP. The first big one was in May 1960, the demonstration against the Un-American Activities Committee hearings in San Francisco, really big, which we've all seen in the famous *Berkeley in the Sixties* film. That was a YPSL/CP collaboration. A number of the trade unions on campus were involved.

Now there were also fights between YPSL and the CP. They were generally for forming trade unions and nobody else was, aside from us. So we collaborated in building the unions even though we had differences. The CP even endorsed one of our pamphlets. I spoke at a Du Bois Club meeting and got them to endorse it. I asked that they come out in support of freeing our comrades in Poland. It was a basic free speech issue. You want to defend the right of communists to have free speech in Berkeley? What about the same right for our comrades in Poland? Some of them went along with it because they were afraid. They were aiming to become a public group, get official status and all that. We were for that, of course. So we had an on-again, off-again relationship. It would always turn off at election time because they were all for voting for the Democrats and we weren't. And that would show up in our union campaign work together.

Tom: Yes, the CP going public. I remember they were effectively

Joel Geier speaking at Socialist Alternative's Marxism conference in Melbourne, 2016

repressed. They wanted to break out of this and if they did something as unpopular as supporting the Polish crackdown, it would make things more difficult for them. But what form would it take to go public?

Joel: Bettina Aptheker, as one of the Free Speech Movement leaders, probably number three or four after Savio and Weinberg, was an extremely popular figure. She was more on the conservative wing of the movement, while we were the left wing of that movement. We co-operated with the CP in the Free Speech Movement; they were the right wing, we were the left wing, but we were in it together making it a success. Anyhow, the CP was going to use Bettina as the vehicle to have public communists – to be able to have communist speakers, who were still banned – on the Berkeley campus. That was their strategy. Use Bettina as a well-known public figure to allow communists to function like anyone else on the campus, to become a legitimate club, make the Du Bois Clubs legitimate. The first communist speaker would have been her father, Herbert Aptheker.

From Berkeley to Australia

Tom: We were fresh from being members of the Berkeley IS when we were instrumental in setting up an organisation in Australia, so we were very heavily influenced in our thinking by our own recent experience. I think the most important thing we brought from the Berkeley IS to the Australian movement was the concept of "socialism from below". Janey always says that the concept and in particular Hal Draper's pamphlet *The Two Souls of Socialism* were very important for her, as she had come from a Communist Party background. When I later started putting together a newsletter for Indonesia, the first article was called "The Two Souls of Socialism". It was the standard way to open an educational.

Robert: And for those of us who came later such as myself, Draper's pamphlet showed how social democracy and Stalinism were pretty much the same thing, namely "socialism from above". I can imagine people coming from either Labor Party backgrounds or Communist Party backgrounds would never have conceived things like that.

Tom: Although we also did bring the "bureaucratic collectivism" line, I think it was really a minor technicality for most people.

But another important thing we brought from the American IS was the idea of rank and file workers' activism. We tried to apply that in our union interventions here. There were people in Australia who wanted to relate to working class politics.

Robert Zocchi
Photo: Robert Zocchi

They were already here. Some of them were at May Day the year we arrived. We ran into people here and there. It wasn't that we recruited workers; we didn't, not significantly anyway. We recruited people who were interested in workers.

Women's liberation and gay liberation were there from day one when we started up in Australia. It was just automatic for us. We arrived in December 1971 and by February 1972 Janey had already initiated a WL group at Melbourne University.

In terms of culture, what represented the most significant transmission from the Berkeley IS to our group in Australia was the *Socialist Songbook* – a whole series of songs which were incredibly popular here for a long period of time, for example *Bill Bailey*: "You may be a comrade to all these folks but you ain't no comrade of mine!"

I thought these songs were pretty funny then, although I might be a bit more restrained about them now. But anyway, we introduced them to Australia and they became very popular.

Joel: One young Australian comrade asked me about Max Shachtman. I ventured to say that a lot of the political ideas in the young comrade's head right now originated with Shachtman. For example: "Neither Washington nor Moscow". It goes back to the Hitler-Stalin Pact and the Nazi invasion of Poland. Do you support the Russians if they invade Poland? That's what the split in the Trotskyist movement was about. That's the origin of the "Neither Washington nor Moscow" slogan. The idea that the British IS took those ideas from America was a big revelation for our young comrades!

Culture and counterculture

Robert: I wanted to ask another question about the relation of IS politics to the counter-culture of that era and place. And furthermore, I wanted to specifically ask Joel, seeing as he joined in 1960, about the relation to the earlier counterculture movements such as the Beats of the 1950s. People like Ginsberg wearing suits and ties, and yet they were bitterly against that society. I bring this up because, as a teenager in the 1970s, I did miss the excitement of this era, I just vaguely remember things on TV. I think I had a rather nostalgic view of the era. But when I read Chris Harman's book *The Fire Last Time*, I realised just how nostalgic my view was, because in fact the real deal revolutionary politics that *were* actually capable of transforming society were still held by a tiny minority within the movements despite the millions of radicals and revolutionaries who existed then throughout the world.

Joel: In the 1950s, the left was so small. We were rebels and the counterculture people were rebels. So there was a crossover. I remember going to hear the first Beat poets when I was a student at someone's house in the 50s. They took their clothes off as they read their poetry! Ginsberg was around the Shachtmanites. He had come out of a Communist family.

As for the counter-culture in the 60s, well, someone like me would have already by then been an old fogey. Except one thing: we were all for drugs! And sex and rock'n'roll! Our attitude was that you go through

Tom reading the *Berkeley Tribe* produced by striking workers from the *Berkeley Barb*

the experiences of your generation. We had no objections to sex, drugs and rock'n'roll. Until people went into countercultural lifestyles, which were so destructive.

Tom: There were definite cultural markers going on in Berkeley, perhaps typical of the period. I had a funny experience at the checkout of a co-operative grocery. They said you could tell there were two kinds of people who would roll up to the checkout – the politicos, and the hippies. For example, people like me – my hair wasn't as short as it is now, but it was, by Berkeley standards, pretty short. So I complained about this. Basically I said it's not fair, just because I have shorter hair you won't take me seriously!

Then there was the newspaper the *Berkeley Barb*. It was a bit trashy, but also had a lot of political news.

Joel: That was put out by Max Scherr. He had been in the CP years before. There were underground newspapers and this was the Berkeley one. He wanted to sell it. He'd always carry them around himself. He put in sex stuff, even a sex columnist – a doctor – who gave good advice. He was a really nice guy, a friend of mine. But the paper also carried all the political news, all the movement activity news.

Janey: I remember one *Berkeley Barb* front page showing someone with an enormous dick and the American flag flying off it!

Joel: That's Berkeley! As we used to say – Berserkeley!

WHAT HAPPENED TO THE SIXTIES?

Socialist Alternative magazine, May 2008

Remembering a magic year like 1968 is bitter-sweet. Where has the magic gone?

We demanded "the immediate recognition, and complete gratification, of all needs and desires". Yet today the planet is stalked by hunger.

The radical movements of those days are no more, and capitalism proved more durable than we hoped.

Yet by no means all the gains of those days were lost. One of the most important was the victory of the Vietnamese people over US imperialism. The National Liberation Front's historic Tet Offensive shattered the myth of American military invincibility, galvanising Western anti-war movements and third world independence movements alike.

America's well-deserved defeat left a legacy called the "Vietnam Syndrome" – people just wouldn't tolerate another war like that one. Ever since then, US presidents have tried desperately to shake off the Syndrome, with little success. Even after the 2001 World Trade Centre attacks, public opinion didn't support George Bush's Iraq war adventure for long.

A second important gain from the sixties was a greater political space to mount opposition movements to whatever evil our rulers cook up. It's hard to believe now that you once needed a permit to leaflet in the Melbourne CBD. Open defiance made this rule a dead letter during the Vietnam era, and attempts to bring it back since then have failed.

Political demonstrations were

widely seen as disreputable until the Vietnam moratorium. But these days almost everyone takes them for granted, with half a million marching against the Iraq invasion in 2003.

Social advances from those days are fundamental to the way we live today. The Women's Liberation Movement did away with social restrictions on the female half of the population that we now look back on with horror – it's staggering to think there was a time they kept women (especially married women) out of a wide range of jobs, not to mention public bars.

The 1969 Stonewall riots in New York sparked an international Gay Liberation Movement. The succeeding decade saw defiant marches in Sydney, giving rise to the Gay and Lesbian Mardi Gras. Today gay marriage is on the agenda.

The counter-culture of the sixties lives on in many forms. It's not just that a few weeks back I saw Barry McGuire on *Spicks and Specks*, singing "The Eve of Destruction". It's the whole flamboyant pop music scene that we take for granted. Hard to believe, isn't it, that once upon a time Elvis couldn't be shown on TV from the waist down?

On the other hand, much has been lost. We can live without Chairman Mao's *Little Red Book*, but where are the radical mass social movements? Feminism today is as much about career networks as it is about changing society. And even with global warming reaching a terrifying stage, there is no mobilisation around environmental issues to compare with the anti-nuclear movements of the seventies and early eighties – which were in some ways the last gasp of the Vietnam-era activists.

Some important gains of the sixties are under savage attack today. Around the world, anti-Muslim hysteria has given governments an excuse to whip up a new racism and cut back civil liberties. In this country, the Howard-Rudd "intervention" into the Northern Territory aims to reverse land rights and other gains made by Indigenous people which had their roots in the sixties.

Basic trade union rights that we won through mass strikes in 1969 were eroded under Malcolm Fraser, indirectly undermined further under Hawke and Keating, then savaged by Howard's ghastly WorkChoices – which Rudd is mostly maintaining.

So what went wrong?

The most important factor was a series of working class defeats. When workers take the offensive, it exposes all the weaknesses of governments and other oppressive social structures. This emboldens other movements of the oppressed. That's what happened in the late sixties and early seventies, as strike levels soared.

But defeats followed in the later seventies and early eighties. These happened in many places: in Britain Margaret Thatcher defeated the coal miners, while in America Ronald Reagan smashed the air traffic controllers' union. In Australia the same thing happened via a long war of attrition.

Australian unions put up fierce resistance to the 1975 sacking of the Whitlam government, then a year later they mobilised general strikes when Malcolm Fraser attacked the Medibank health scheme. 1977 saw a huge power workers' dispute in the Latrobe Valley in defiance of the state government. As late as 1981 the country was in the grip of a strike wave.

But the earlier struggles ended in disappointment, because the union leaders were looking for industrial peace rather than victory. There were militant rank and file networks that did fight to win, and these had achieved victories in earlier years, but by 1975 mass unemployment was weakening their bargaining position. The 1981 strike wave achieved gains in wages and hours, but it didn't have the political cutting edge of the earlier actions. After years of industrial battles, worker militants were tired and bruised.

Then came the Hawke-Keating era of Labor governments. They paid lip service to progressive causes, and their Accord with the unions put ACTU bureaucrats like Bill Kelty in positions of power. But Hawke and Kelty used "consensus" around the Accord to undermine worker activism and force wages down. By the time John Howard defeated Labor in 1996, the unions were vastly weakened and Howard could kick heads.

As organised labour retreated, social movements lost confidence. For example, the union connection was important for Aborigines. As the Black women's paper *Koori-Bina* put it during the struggle against uranium mining:

> We must…enlist the support of the white Australian working class culminating in union action to prevent the destruction of our lands. It was from the unions that the Gurindjis obtained their greatest support… The Land Councils are aware of the critical need for union support and have asked supporters in the southern cities to ask for union bans.

Tom speaking on Sproul Hall steps in Berkeley 2012 to an imaginary crowd. In reality the closest thing to a crowd was a series of fraternities collecting applications for membership at tables where the left used to set up

This hope no longer seemed realistic by the 1990s.

The decline in class struggle affected other movements too. International Women's Day had been a working women's day. By the nineties it was better known as an occasion for business lunches. And with industrial trade unionism on the back foot, it's hardly surprising governments decided to smash student unions.

Driven by these social trends, people's ideas also drifted rightwards over the years, diverting social criticism into the bog of post-modernism, and portraying the free market as an economic answer to everything.

But this trend has now turned around. Over the past two decades, opinion polls have shown Australians returning to more left wing values – they want higher spending on education and health, and they worry about rising inequality. Pollster Mary Winter reported: "Most people see big business as a ruthless, money-making machine".

People are scrapping right wing ideas, because they're fed up with working harder for lousy pay, with prejudice and discrimination, and with environmental destruction. Of course it's still a big step from mass dissatisfaction to mass struggle. We can't say when large numbers will take that step. But take it they will. And when that day comes, they'll look to the sixties for inspiration.

GARBAGE STRIKE IN MISSISSIPPI

In the northern summer of 1971, Janey and I travelled to the American South. After visiting the bright lights of New Orleans, we arrived in Jackson, Mississippi on a Greyhound bus at dusk.

It was only a few years since the end of segregation, and there was still the odd sign saying "Whites only". Walking through the city, we crossed an invisible boundary, and suddenly there was a load of garbage in the streets. Right next door the streets were clean. Could the difference between white and Black be so stark? Yes it could, when Black garbage workers were on strike. Black residents refused to scab, and paid the price. We were keen to meet some of the activists who were supporting the garbage workers and made our way to the union office.

We sat in on a meeting, and introduced ourselves. Going for dinner afterwards to a hamburger restaurant with some northern activists, we experienced the edge of racist reality. We were a group of five, including a Black guy (the only one in the restaurant), two obvious northerners (me and a guy from New York) with beards, and two women in short skirts. They didn't dare not serve us, but we did have to wait for a long time with everyone staring at us.

Our new friends told us about an upcoming political event. Medgar Evers, who was a Black civil rights advocate from Mississippi, had been assassinated in 1963, as told in Bob Dylan's song "Only a pawn in their game". His brother Charles Evers was in 1971 the mayor of Fayette, Mississippi. He was the first Black

Postcard from Jackson Mississippi, 1971

mayor in the state and had recently been re-elected.

We drove to Fayette to see him inaugurated, and witnessed an astonishing political meeting. Instead of a conventional (to us) political speech, Evers made his inaugural speech in the style of a Black preacher, with a chorus of singers humming along in the background. After meeting the mayor, we drove back right through a hurricane, afraid our car would be swept away in the howling winds and rain. We did make it back safely to Jackson and lived to continue the struggle another day. But we will never forget that unique political meeting.

85 **Garbage strike in Mississippi**

Clockwise from top: Tom and Janey with representative of Kakumaru Tokyo September 1971; Tom at Byodo-in Temple, Kyoto; Tom on the balcony of a ryokan (Japanese style inn) in Tokyo; Tom with a representative of Kakumaru

REVOLUTIONARIES IN SUITS: JAPAN 1971

Leaving the US to go to Australia in September 1971, we went first to Japan. Janey and I had met some Japanese-American political activists at Berkeley. Two or three of them were ethnic Japanese, but as US citizens they could have been expelled from Japan. The group was very sophisticated politically and intellectually, and gave us a certain perspective on Japan. The key figure was Don Philippi, who was not himself Japanese. He worked as a professional translator and was expert in a classical Japanese musical instrument. An amazing intellect.

The left in Japan at the time had a general orientation to direct action. A major issue was the construction of the new Narita Airport which had involved confrontations between 10,000 riot police and a similar number of students and farmers over three months in 1968.

Although my father and his family had intimate associations with Asia, and I had grown up with this connection, this was my first direct experience with the region.

Don organised for us to meet some political contacts in Tokyo. One of them met us at the airport, put us up in a friend's flat, and also showed

Tom wearing a Japanese jacket, 1971

us around Tokyo. He arranged for us to have discussions with leaders and prominent members of the Kakumaru (Japan Revolutionary Communist League), an organisation with perhaps 5,000 members. They were active in campus organising. The comrades turned up with a plate of sushi, wearing suits and ties, which to someone fresh from the counter-culture atmosphere in Berkeley was a bit unexpected.

During the meeting I referred to "socialist democracy". This was a Shachtmanite expression I had picked up in Berkeley, democracy being at the core of everything. But when I said we believed in socialist democracy, the Japanese leader understood me as saying that I believed in *social* democracy, this bringing forth a thundering reply. We had to clarify – no, no, no, we weren't social democrats.

We found meeting these activists enlightening, an opportunity to relate to politics in Japan, and not just be tourists. We had chosen the Kakumaru simply because we had the contacts. However, it is clear to me that they were essentially ultra-left extremists. If I could turn the clock back I would choose to meet members of Chukaku, a breakaway party from the Japanese Communist Party, who had some sympathy for Trotskyism.

After Japan, we travelled through Hong Kong and South-East Asia. In Malaysia we met a contractor who informed us that Australians were "lazy", by which he seemed to mean they were militant. Anyway he got an earful. I hadn't yet got to Australia, but I was already defending working class militancy.

I.S. IN AUSTRALIA: THE EARLY DAYS

We landed in Sydney in December 1971. Before flying on to Melbourne we spent a couple of hours in Manly, where a well-tanned young athlete ran past us to the kiosk, calling out "a pie and chips, thanks": here was a classic introduction to Australia.

As we had just come from three months in Asia, south-eastern Australia in general didn't seem that different from the US to me. It was surprisingly a lot like California. Politically, I was struck at how collectivist the left was here and was impressed with the automatic orientation to the labour movement I noticed in Australia. Although things have changed, to a degree that is still with us.

It was automatic for us to immediately go looking for the left. We found it first in the new offices of the SYA (Socialist Youth Alliance) and John Percy, who Janey already knew from university days. John was friendly as always. We spent some time around the SYA, going to their meetings and talking to them. I remember saying I was going to try to split them. But Janey didn't approve; she thought that was ultra-left.

The SYA had distinguished themselves in the student movement. They came out of Sydney primarily, which is where most Trotskyists were. Jim Percy, John's brother, led the group. They managed to put out a fortnightly paper, which later went weekly.

I argued with them over the Russian question. They held the position that the USSR was a degenerated workers' state, whereas we contended it was not in any way

a workers' state. Coming from the American IS current, we adhered to a theory which designated the Stalinist society "bureaucratic collectivism". The argument that Russia was *not* some kind of workers' state, *not* some form of socialism, however distorted or degenerated, was new to them, and led to a lot of discussion.

Then on May Day 1972, marching through Melbourne to the Yarra Bank, we met people who would shape our revolutionary lives.

The new acquaintances were a group of people called the Marxist Workers Group, around Monash student Dave Nadel. What attracted me about the MWG was the working class politics. The broadsheet we got from them that May Day has remained in our memories in slightly different ways. Janey remembers a cartoon by Mark Matcott, which reminded us of the style of the Berkeley IS. I remember the word "crisis" repeated several times, followed by an argument that the working class needed a program to face this.

Janey knew some of the members of this group too, including Dave and also Chris Gaffney. Prior to the formation of the MWG, Dave and Chris had been in a group called Tocsin, whose focus was a traditional Trotskyist view of the working class. They had been influenced by Ted

Tripp, an old Trotskyist, but they had had bad experiences with another Trotskyist group.

Dave didn't have any strong overseas models. As a whole, by the time we encountered them, MWG did not seem to be going anywhere, but there were individuals in it who were trying to work things out. We started going to their meetings, and in the process got Dave interested in the IS Tendency. Other people we related to in this group were Tess Lee Ack, Mark Matcott and Phil Griffiths.

A significant incident occurred around a member who saw himself as representing blue collar workers in the group – he emphasised his Australian accent, swore a lot and would guilt trip the students for their middle class origins. As part of pushing his working class persona, he made sexist and racist remarks. At one meeting very soon after we started attending, he used a racist term referring to Tess. Janey and I had been schooled in the meetings of the Berkeley IS. Black Power was right at the doorstep, women's liberation and gay liberation had just emerged.

Tom on ferry in Sydney Harbour on the day of his arrival to Australia November 1971; Mike Grewcock; Dave Nadel, photo provided by Dave; (opposite page) SWAG members and others on International Women's Day demonstration 1973, left to right: unknown, Silvie Leber, Dilys Kevan, Janey Stone, Rose Stone (Janey's mother), unknown, Tess Lee Ack

You absolutely would challenge any racism, sexism and homophobia on the spot. When Janey objected to the remark, one member tried to say that it was really quite alright because it was meant in a humorous manner and that Tess didn't mind anyway. But

I.S. in Australia: the early days

The Battler
Issue No1
November 1972

Tess spoke up "Actually, I do mind!" At that point everybody realised you could actually stand up to this guy.

Although I subscribed to the theory of bureaucratic collectivism as an analysis of Russia, that wasn't the most important political issue. Leninism and the nature of the organisation we were trying to build were way more important. We set up a faction called Red Ink which polarised things, and after some time the MWG moved from being eclectic to a group that was more homogeneous.

Red Ink initially contained Janey and me, Dave, Tess and Mark. We wanted incipient leaders, not just people who happened to agree with us. Griff was the sixth, after he developed from his original libertarian politics. In the following year, we added Ross McKenzie, a newly arrived Scot, and Jeff Goldhar, an Australian, both of whom had been members of the British IS. It was a matter of assembling forces that were of an IS frame of mind. We always hoped more people would come from Britain, but few ever did.

Around the end of 1972, we got tired of being asked "how many Marxist workers do you have?", and changed the name to SWAG (Socialist Workers Action Group). We wanted a name that would not be too pretentious. But although the short version had a friendly sound, the full name was hardly more modest than the earlier one. The name has been perceived as nationalist but it was more that we were trying to be "folksy" to sound local and familiar to people in Australia. Our literature service, Jumbooks, and the name Red Ink were in the same spirit.

With the 1972 elections approaching, we decided to produce a newspaper. Dave was keen to call it *The Battler*, which he argued for on the basis of Australian cultural references I couldn't judge – so I agreed to it. It was an odd name, and some people laughed at it, but on balance it didn't do us any harm and workers felt quite comfortable with it. The main value of this first issue of *The Battler*, however, was to prove to us we weren't ready to publish a paper. The front page headline was as follows, the first line in a tiny font, and the second larger:

A vote for Labor is the first step to

FIGHT THE LABOR LEADERS.

Although we were for a change of government, we wanted to criticise Labor and warn of betrayals to come. But amidst the euphoric Whitlam

THE BATTLER

NOVEMBER 17, 1972   VOL. I NO. 1   TEN CENTS

A VOTE FOR LABOR IS THE FIRST STEP TO

FIGHT THE LABOR LEADERS!

All around Melbourne, car stickers and T-shirts scream: "It's Time". The Herald produces banner headlines for each optimistic utterance of the Liberal Party cabinet. It's easy to see there is an election on. More interest and urgency has been created around this election, than at any time since 1949. But with Labor selling itself on gimmicks, and Whitlam reluctant to publicise his policies, we must be tempted to ask ourselves: "Does it really matter? Is there any difference anyway?" The Battler believes that there is a difference, and that this election does matter, though not for the reasons that Gough Whitlam would have us believe.

The coming Federal election is the most important in the last twenty-five years. It takes place in a period of increasing economic crisis, growing working class and indeed general militancy and discontent, and of confusion and defeat in world affairs for the imperialist powers -- and therefore for the Australian ruling class. It will almost certainly lead to the election of a Labor government. Therefore no socialist group which orients to the working class can ignore the elections. For all workers there are only two real choices: a vote for Labor or a boycott of the elections. Socialists must declare themselves one way or the other. To ignore the elections is to ignore the political struggles of the working class.

We are for Labor but we have no illusions. The Labor Party cannot solve the crisis that will lead to its election. It neither wishes to, nor knows how. But the Labor Party can be forced to defend the basic interests of the working class in a way that the Liberals cannot. The Liberals as an open party of big business can only be fought industrially. Labor, though it serves capitalism, depends on the working class for its political existence, and can be fought by its rank-and-file and the Trade Union movement. We can win certain basic demands from the Labor Party, but only if we fight them. To do it we need to build a mass movement inside and outside the ALP to force the Labor leadership to defend the working class. The roots of such a movement exist in such bodies as the Socialist Left and the Rebel Unions but they can only become effective if there is a real mobilisation of the rank-and-file inside them.

Continued on page 5

SOCIALIST WORKERS' ACTION

EDITORIAL

The 1970's bring the beginnings of a social crisis to Australia, a crisis which already grips most of the world. It has its roots in the social system under which we live, a system that puts the means of production, and the institutions that control people's lives, in the hands of a small group of rich exploiters, who run society not for the good of all but for private profit. That profit in turn is created out of the exploitation of the working class. To maintain that exploitation and supplement it overseas, the Australian ruling class in the 1970's is attacking the jobs and wages of workers, and trying to build up a "mini-imperialism" in the Pacific Region. To keep its opponents among themselves, it fosters poisonous divisions in society along racial, ethnic and sex lines, and an ugly national chauvinism.

As the crisis develops, it poses new questions to the Australian working class and to the left-wing organisations. For workers it points to the need for new strategies to fight the bosses, and for a new understanding of society. For radicals and socialists, it creates the possibility for the first time in many years of building a left-wing movement inside the working class: in its political organisations and ultimately in factories, offices and transport, where the strength of the organised working class lies. The transition from the glamour of the protest to the hard slogging of industrial work is not an easy one, but that is all the more reason why we should begin to consider it now.

SOCIALIST WORKERS' ACTION is still developing its positions on many political questions. It grew out of an awareness that there was a vacuum on the Left: a need for organisations which would begin the turn to the working class, the urgent task of revolutionaries in the 1970's. Inseparable from a growing pro-working class orientation is the clear understanding of the anti-working class character of the so-called "Communist" regimes in both Moscow and Peking. If we are to build a workers' movement to overthrow capitalism, we cannot afford to be tied emotionally and politically to bureaucratic regimes. We view ourselves as making some first steps toward the creation of a *revolutionary socialist workers' movement, in opposition to both bankrupt reformism and repressive stalinism.* That is the only force that can create a world free of oppression and exploitation.

SOCIALIST WORKERS' ACTION is not, at this time, a disciplined organisation, and THE BATTLER is not a "political line" newspaper. Signed articles, therefore, do not necessarily represent the views of THE BATTLER, SWA, or of the publisher.

PAPER OF THE SOCIALIST WORKERS' ACTION GROUP

Volume 1, Number 1
10cents

stuff their cars...
WHAT ABOUT OUR JOBS?

IS THE GOVERNMENT'S handling of the British Leyland collapse a guide line for future victims of the recession? Leyland is not the first company to get itself into trouble this year. It won't be the last. At Zetland (Sydney) last week the government effectively said "damn the workers, we're going to help the company." Is this a precedent?

Of course, Kep Enderby, Minister for Manufacturing, tells it differently. He argues that if the government hadn't spent $25 million buying the factory site and 782 Leyland cars then Leyland would have had to close completely and the 9000-plus workers involved in making buses and assembling Mini's would have lost their jobs as well. Garbage! Buses and Mini's are profitable. P76's and Marinas weren't. Besides, Enderby's proposals do nothing for the 3,000 and more workers who are going to lose their jobs at Leyland, not to mention the many other workers in industries supplying component parts to Leyland.

Joe Thompson, NSW secretary of Vehicle Builders' Employees Federation, came up with a much better proposal for Leyland's wreckage. He thinks it should be nationalised. We agree. He also said that the government should buy the factory (as a factory rather than a housing site) from Leyland. We don't agree. We

don't think we should have to BUY it from our taxes. Australian workers didn't design the ridiculous P76! Thompson has also advised Leyland workers to resist dismissal. Not to leave the factory when it closes. At the time of going to press it isn't clear whether this is going to happen,

but it ought to. That is the real way to fight the sackings. Push for nationalisation -- without any compensation -- <u>under workers' control</u>.

To get this means a fight, and at this stage its unlikely that the VBEF is prepared The Labor Government may be able to get away with making a present to British Leyland We must be organised to make sure they don't make present of our future next time a company fails.

Harold Wilson's
SOCIAL CON-TRICK

HAROLD WILSON and his Social Contract have just been re-elected in Britain. British workers have a pretty fair idea of what this means for their living standards, but the result of these elections will be felt in Australia too.

Mind you, it wasn't much of a victory. Labour has a 3-seat majority and got its second lowest percentage of the vote in the last ten elections! The British working class voted Labour because all the other parties were explicitly anti-working class. Unionists aren't going to vote for parties running on a "bash the unions" platform!

But Labour's win doesn't mean an end to the attack on workers' living standards -- there's a deepening economic crisis in Britain, and the only way out for the ruling class is to attack workers. The Tories did this, and Labour has different ways of doing the same thing. But having Labour in office means that the fight can and will shift to the factories and offices, and to the internal life of the trade unions. It means that the growing rank and file groups of workers in Britain will have to concentrate on smashing the Social Contract <u>at their places of work</u>.

The Social Contract -- or Con-Trick, as radical British workers call it -- is an agreement between the Labour government and Labour-supporting unions (some of which are led by members of the British Communist Party) to hold down wages. Under the Con-Trick, wage rises are guaranteed, but they are less than the rate at which prices rise. These agreements would operate for at least twelve months. The idea behind the Con-Trick is that workers are supposed to be able to rely on getting wage rises <u>without</u> taking industrial action which disrupts productivity.

The point is, of course, that under these conditions, the rises never <u>are</u> fair.

If all of this sounds like Australian Labor Minister Cameron's proposals on wage indexation, it's no coincidence. The fact that Wilson won an election on the Social Contract and was able to get co-operation from "Left" trade union leaders will not go unnoticed in Canberra. Australia has an economic crisis of its own. It's not as bad as Britain's, but it's getting worse. Cameron, Crean and Cairns are going all out to sell wage indexation as an alternative to conventional deflation strategy. Conventional strategy has already caused the worst unemployment in Australia since 1946.

turn to back page

inside

Behind the Mainline Crash
...centre pages

Sackings in Insurance
...page 2

Cops called at Monash
...page 3

W.A. General Strike
...back page

campaign of 1972, making your central message the need to fight the Labor leaders was sectarian. Read from any distance only the second line was legible: the paper might have been taken for a conservative publication.

But in any case we couldn't keep up publication with such a small number of people. When we started up *The Battler* again two years later we began again with number one, so there are actually TWO *Battler* Number Ones.

As a group of about 12 people what we could do was obviously very limited. But we did manage to get some presence with our broadsheets, mostly distributed on campus. They were typed up and reproduced on a Gestetner duplicator. I had learnt typing in high school in America, so I became our chief typist.

We had four articles on two sides of one sheet of paper, and because we had no money and so little printing space, we had to be very concise and to the point. I contributed significantly to developing our writing style. Dave Nadel, who had significant experience in editing publications and reducing verbiage to fit it all into a paragraph, was also very important in teaching people how to write. Phil Griffiths also made a major contribution. Phil says in the Acknowledgements of his PhD thesis that Dave Nadel and I taught him how to write. I would say that the reverse is also true.

We also managed to put out several issues of a journal, which allowed for somewhat longer articles. Three issues of *Front Line* came out in 1974, with further issues appearing sporadically over the next couple of years. In 1979 the name was changed to *International Socialist*.

Our situation in SWAG at the time forms a sharp contrast with that of the SYA/SWL (Socialist Youth Alliance/ Socialist Workers League) who were putting out *Direct Action*, a full newspaper. Because they had much more money and therefore space, they

SWAG and friends lining up in Drummond St Mayday 1974. Left to right: Kevin Bain, Roger Molombey, Mike Grewcock (at back), Phil Ilton, unknown, Tom O'Lincoln; (opposite page) *The Battler* Issue No1 October 1974

I.S. in Australia: the early days

Mick Armstrong; (left to right) Graham Smith, Dave Nadel, Kevin Bain, Tom O'Lincoln in Palmerston St Carlton 1974; Alec Kahn; (opposite page) Terry O'Lincoln (left), Ross McKenzie (right) on the roof of the Pram Factory Lygon St Carlton, 1973

could write much more at length.

In spite of our tiny size, we were able to win serious activists to our IS politics. Apart from whatever powers of persuasion we had, our success was only possible in the context of the dramatic social radicalisation and surge of class struggle in Australia and internationally between 1967 and 1974. At the same time, the monolithic hold of Stalinist Communist Parties and reformist Labor and Social Democratic Parties on both the left and the working class was weakening. Partly this was due to high levels of class struggle. Radical students were contemptuous of the moderate politics of the Communist Party and hostile to the Soviet regime; and in Australia, after Labor's defeat in 1966, large numbers turned from Laborism to direct action.

All these factors helped shape the development of our small organisation. The high levels of class struggle made our theoretical argument for a working class orientation credible, and presented opportunities for practical interventions in picket lines and mass meetings. The campus radicalisation was where most of our new members came from. It is easier for a small group to recruit students, as they can be convinced on the basis of ideas. Dissatisfaction with existing parties made it easier to argue for building a new type of

96   I.S. in Australia: the early days

political organisation.

At Monash we were centrally involved in a student club called the Revolutionary Communists (RevComms), which produced a weekly leaflet called *Hard Lines*. There was a core of people who were members of the parent organisation, while others were more of a periphery.

In 1974 Tess Lee Ack led 150 students in occupying the university administration building for a week. The occupation had extremely radical demands, including the abolition of competitive assessment, student-staff control of course content, and open admissions to allow the entry of more working class students.

Dave Nadel, a leader of the Labor Club at an earlier stage, returned to Monash in a mentoring role and was also essential for advancing specifically Marxist arguments to push the struggle leftwards.

This was not as big as previous occupations, but it was more prolonged. The action was one of the last major struggles of the student movement which had begun in the late sixties. It showed that the movement was in decline but had an activist element demonstrating considerable maturity. SWAG recruited some leading activists and we grew from 15 to 25 members, which made it possible to re-launch *The Battler*

and sustain it as a monthly.

We also recruited Mick Armstrong from La Trobe during this period. Mick made his mark very quickly.

He was attacked by the Maoists during a dispute over who should be a delegate to an Australian Union of Students conference. The Maoists had been outmanoeuvred, so they claimed it was not a legitimate delegation and said they would kick him out.

They were running across tables at the conference, physically attacking Mick, trying to drive him out of the conference. It was nerve-wracking and scary - you didn't know what they were going to do. But Mick was right there in the middle of it all, cool as a cucumber. So the next day we mobilised about a dozen people to go out and defend Mick against these attacks. And that number was enough to succeed – you can see how few people were actually involved.

Another member from this period I would like to mention is Jeff Goldhar. One time there was a Timor demonstration on the steps of the Melbourne GPO at the corner of Elizabeth and Bourke Streets before Bourke Street became a mall. The cops arrived and said "Get off". Jeff,

Terry, Tom and Janey on roof of Pram Factory, Lygon Street Carlton 1973; Jeff Goldhar; Phil Griffiths with Janey September 2015

a lawyer by training, pointed out that as it was the GPO, we were covered by commonwealth not state jurisdiction. As a state instrumentality, the police had no jurisdiction on GPO property! Jeff proceeded to march them off, leaving us in possession.

I remember another incident involving Jeff, at a demonstration where there was some physical confrontation. A guy right in front of Jeff was about to dash into the fray, but Jeff just grabbed him by the hair and pulled him back. I was impressed, because Jeff never struck you as a great physical fighter or anything, but he had courage and was smart.

Jeff died at a young age in 1997. In his will, he left a bequest to be used for socialist projects, to "allow us to bring our history and ideas to those receptive to them".

> I would think about the past and how our history was disappearing. We have a proud history... I'd like our history to be remembered. I'd like our ideas to be available.

Jeff's bequest allowed the publication of an impressive list of books, including several of my own. And this book of memoirs is in fact the last to be published using money from his bequest.

Alec Kahn, who had been involved with the RevComms during the Monash occupation in 1974, joined SWAG in 1975. Alec made a major contribution to *Hard Lines*, and subsequently to *The Battler*. In my view Alec was the best left journalist of his era in Australia, and as good as anything internationally. He was equally good at teaching people how to write. Some of his *Battler* front covers are classic. He also wrote great content. Alec's mind always ticking over, and he was always up for an intellectual challenge in difficult situations.

A special talent he had was to play his role as journalist while he was involved in industrial disputes, for example, when he went to the Latrobe Valley east of Melbourne to cover a major strike by power workers there in 1977. Alec was great on picket lines, much liked by the workers, and he combined journalism with actual industrial organising and strike support work. Because of this, important insights about such a major industrial dispute were preserved for posterity. He also knew what were the right questions to ask because of his strong politics.

Mark Matcott made an enormous contribution to *Hard Lines* and *The Battler* with his brilliant cartoons. He was a professional quality car-

victory for the Prime Minister rather than a political victory for the labor *movement* -- because Whitlam wants to be independent of his rank and file.

Mark Matcott cartoon on SWAG election flyer, 1974 showing Gough Whitlam, Bob Menzies and Bill Sneddon; Mark Matcott cartoon; *Front Line* Issue No1 May 1974 featuring cartoon by Mark Matcott

toonist and gave a dimension to the organisation that nobody else could provide. In particular with our early efforts with the newspaper, Mark often rescued us with a great cartoon.

Mark was an original character. There was a bit of an attitude on the left generally that the class struggle was too serious to be treated humorously, for example, in cartoons. Mark's humour made political points as sharply as anything.

Dave Nadel was an indispensable figure in the early life of the organisation. We would never have got anywhere if it hadn't been for Dave. The RevComms wouldn't have happened without him and because of him the paper was a huge success. Griff had a madcap approach to it which contributed a lot but it was also the solid politics of Dave Nadel that made it so effective.

When he left the organisation he made it clear he wanted to remain friends, but I ignored the signal, because all I could think about was building the organisation. I have regretted that ever since.

Phil Griffiths is quite difficult to characterise. He is an iconoclast. He liked to challenge ideas and this was evident in how he worked in the newspaper. I remember the headline about the "one time two time trade union officials" which nearly got him sued. On another occasion he was threatened with legal action by Botany Council in Sydney.

SWAG existed for three years from December 1972 to 1975 and this was really the first phase of the development of our tendency in Australia.

The period when Janey and I were overseas for six months in 1975 can be considered a second phase. While we were away, Dave and Griff led the group. *The Battler* had been appearing regularly for over a year and they were able to keep producing it while we were away, and show it was not reliant upon us. They sent copies to us at a series of destinations. It was pretty amazing to go to the Poste Restante office in places such as New Delhi and Kabul and receive *The Battler*.

Apart from newspaper production, there were many problems with holding together a small activist group with limited resources. Dave and Griff came out of the whole experience a lot stronger and more confident. When Janey and I returned from our trip at the end of 1975, we were all flung headlong into the mass activities around the dismissal of Whitlam and the creation of a new, larger and more national organisation. We were ready for the third phase of our early development.

"GIMME YOUR PASSPORT!": PORTUGAL 1975

Revolutions are remarkably complex. Books and other people's views and experiences are essential to understand them. But a visit to a country gives you an insight and a feel.

Janey and I spent a couple of weeks in the UK in July 1975, orienting ourselves before we went to Portugal. One day we went to a party. Somebody came up to us and said, "Are you going to Portugal?" I said "Yes". "Have you got a passport?" "Yes." "Gimme your passport!"

This was Tony Cliff, the leader of the British Socialist Workers Party (SWP)! He was busting to get to the front line of the revolution, but, as a stateless Jew from Palestine, he was unable to travel outside Britain. So he was prepared to unsettle this new comrade who had just arrived.

Joel Geier claims that the Portuguese revolutionary organisation PRP actually offered to smuggle Cliff into Portugal and he was quite flattered. They said "Come, we want you for advice". But in the end he decided it was too dangerous, as he might never be able to get back into Britain. He really wanted to go, but since he had no papers, he was worried he would not be able to return and resume the role he was playing in Britain.

Instead of borrowing my passport, Cliff gathered information from the hundreds of SWP members who visited Portugal over the two years of upheaval, including 54 members who at his request wrote reports after visiting in August 1975. He synthesised this material into an impressive account of the revolution,

Portugal at the Crossroads, published in September 1975, while events were still current.

Since 1932, Portugal had been run by a vicious fascist regime under the dictator Salazar, who was succeeded by Caetano in 1968. By 1974 Portugal was the least developed country in Western Europe. Attempts to build the economy with injections of capital had created social contradictions, with the working class growing substantially due to the boost from foreign funds, alongside a continuing small and backward local capitalist class. Thousands of workers learned the latest industrial techniques at large enterprises like the Lisnave and Setenave shipyards. They learned the most radical politics, too. Even a majority of capitalists were disgruntled and dissatisfied with the state of things.

At the same time Lisbon continued to cling to the last of the great colonial empires in Africa and in Asia (including East Timor). It was fighting wars to keep this empire, and losing. This military fiasco had a destabilising effect on the armed forces, particularly on the middle level officers.

The Portuguese Revolution had begun at 25 minutes past midnight

Revolution, paper of the PRP-BR, 22 August 1975, mass united demonstration of workers, peasants, soldiers and sailers, 21 August 1975

Coverage in *The Battler*; (opposite page) *Republica* 31 July 1975: "The enemies of the people want to destroy the newspaper of the people"

on 25 April 1974, the signal being the popular tune "*Grandola Vila Morena*" ("Grandola brown village in a land of brotherhood"). When the song, which was banned by the dictatorship, was played on radio, a grouping of 400 officers, the Armed Forces Movement (MFA), moved to overthrow Caetano.

The new president General Spínola aimed simply to renovate state power. But demands to "introduce the revolution" into the workplaces created a huge space for working class struggles and protest movements. The subsequent strike wave included nearly every major group of workers, and by May over 2,000,000 workers were on strike across key industries, including shipbuilding, mining, textiles, electronics, hotel and catering and banking.

With the strike wave and the economic instability there was a burst of factory occupations. A typical situation would be where the boss took all the cash out of the system and moved across into Spain, intending to wait it out. This forced the workers to take over control of the factory, like it or not. That happened in 158 workplaces, and in four of them the workers not only took over the workplace but also held managers captive.

In June 1974, the government set up a new military force, called Continental Operations Command (COPCON), hoping it would be more reliable than the radicalised army. But COPCON itself radicalised and often refused to act against workers.

The scale of workers' activity led to two attempted coups. The first, in September 1974, was thwarted when workers mobilised, blocking roads and transport. Soldiers joined a large demonstration in central Lisbon, resulting in a convincing example of working class power. Spínola's intended counter-demonstration of the "silent majority" never happened. A second attempted coup in March 1975 was also a miserable failure.

Workers in the saddle

Janey and I arrived in August 1975, at what was perhaps the high point of the revolutionary wave.

People sometimes ask what it was like to be in a city where, to quote George Orwell, the working class was in the saddle. Well at first glance it seemed to us a bit like Brunswick or Newtown in Australia, or the Mission District in San Francisco – there were posters everywhere! The extent of public debate was also astonishing.

Chris Harman describes the ferment:

> Foreign socialists who visited Lisbon in the summer of 1975 underwent an experience that they would not forget. Here was a city where the majority of the working class wanted socialism and where the old obstacles, in terms of the police, the army and even a well-organized capitalist class, seemed in complete disarray.[11]

As one of those foreign socialists, I have never been anywhere where it was so easy to find revolutionaries. If you dropped into the Lisbon

105 "Gimme your passport!": Portugal 1975

tourist information office they gave you a list of left and revolutionary organisations, complete with name, address and phone numbers. There were dozens of bookstalls in the centre of town. It looked like a university open day, but the bookstalls, selling things like Marx and Lenin, were doing a brisk trade among ordinary people, not just students. There was a fantastic thirst for knowledge, especially for Marxism.

Travelling by train from Lisbon to the seaside suburb of Estoril, we saw an unassuming notice in the ticket booth announcing that prices would be reduced so that working class people could afford to go to the beach. There were no police in the streets. Correction: I once saw two of them down a back alley. They made no attempt to put their stamp on city life.

The factory occupations were of course an attraction for us. We international activists had the striking experience of chatting with insurgent Portuguese workers in board rooms. We visited one of these on the fringes of Lisbon and had a debate about whether Russia was socialist or state capitalist.

Employees at one of the main newspapers, *Diario de Republica*, whose manager was aligned with the Socialist Party, seized control of production and began to run it under workers' control. This was a very contentious action on the left. Was this a Stalinist/MFA attack on free speech? The workers' argument was that the boss was silenced because he represented the class enemy, and that this was normal in an industrial dispute.

This made sense, but I wanted to look further into the issue. I went to the paper's headquarters and read some back issues. From this it was clear to me that the workers' council running the place was not dominated by the Communist Party, as critics claimed, but led by a diversity of activists – and the same went for the general news coverage. The workers' council's first major statement was in fact critical of the MFA and the CP.

The Portuguese far left had grown in the final years of the dictatorship, then had bloomed into numerous competing organisations. None of the revolutionary groups had our politics, but the most promising to us in the IS tendency was the Revolutionary Party of the Proletariat (PRP), which had a mixture of guerrillaist and revolutionary socialist ideas. They had built a strong relationship with the leftward moving soldiers and even officers. Their lack of a clear Leninist

Diario de Noticias 21 August 1975: "Revolutionary support for COPCON in the voice of thousands of workers"

perspective on the other hand was a serious weakness.

There were several Maoist groups. The MRPP (Reorganised Movement of the Party of the Proletariat), which had been very active under Caetano, was noticeably sectarian, having marched on May Day in isolation.

Confronting the revolutionary left was the Portuguese Communist Party (PCP) with its top-down methods, collaborationist politics, and orientation to restraining those who wanted to fight. Some of its members turned from the PCP to the far left. Others, however turned to the Socialist Party, established in 1973 by exiles in Germany. They made militant noises in the early days, then after a resounding success in the March 1975 elections for a constitutional assembly, they also proved a serious alternative draw on working class allegiance.

"Gimme your passport!": Portugal 1975

Two mass marches

In August 1975, the crisis reached a peak with the "Battle of the Documents". Nine senior officers issued a document calling for restraint and acceptance of the constitutional assembly. In response, COPCON published a manifesto with a much more left wing orientation.

> A revolutionary program to resolve the present situation must first of all carry out the alliance between the MFA and the people which guarantees the leadership of the workers... It is necessary to set up a structure of popular mass organisations [that] will have to be...authentic organs of political power...

The far left and rank and file shop stewards called for a demonstration in support of COPCON. The PCP opposed this as too extreme. But sentiment among the militants was too strong and the PCP was ultimately forced to back the march. The scene was set for a political battle on the demonstration when it took place on 20 August.

This demonstration was an amazing experience for us. The enormous march snaked through the poor and working class areas of central Lisbon; all sorts of ordinary people came out of their houses to watch and support the marchers.

Different contingents waged verbal tug-of-war over the slogans. We were part of a far left contingent chanting "Revolutionary United Front!", while the marchers next to us were yelling a more moderate slogan "People's United Front". We got further lessons in Portuguese, as we chanted this and other slogans for hours.

Soldiers and sailors led the march, but they were a small detachment and not armed. In spite of its political limitations, this demonstration was a mass militant action which pulled the Lisbon political scene to the left. The potential still existed to take the revolution forward. But the PCP continued its undermining work.

The follow-up march a week later on 27 August was carefully designed to take the cutting edge off things. Where the first demonstration marched through the centre of town, this one marched away from the centre. Where the first march was full of red banners, this one featured coloured balloons. Where the first one had revolutionary speakers, the second had conventional politicians and we were offered no revolutionary slogans.

That final week in August was the last great high point of the revolution, and due to the Communist Party it drowned in ambiguity. Tony Cliff wrote in September, "Portugal, the weakest link in the capitalist chain in Europe, can become the launching pad for the socialist revolution in the whole of the continent"; but by the time this appeared in print it was already too late.

The right wing sensed its opportunity. On 24 November Otelo de Carvalho, who had played a strategic role in the revolution and was subsequently the leader of COPCON, was removed from his command positions. Younger officers begged him to defy the order, but he refused. The lack of a coherent, sizeable revolutionary party now became evident. There was resistance all over Lisbon, but it was fragmentary and directionless. The revolution began to dissipate.

Chris Harman concluded that the left had been disarmed because "the workers looked to the armed forces to act for them, and inside the armed forces the rank and file looked to the progressive officers for a lead".[12]

Ultimately the big winner was the Socialist Party. Its leader Mario Soares became prime minister in the first regular elections. A vast social upheaval which had opened up some possibilities for socialism subsided into a democratic election within capitalism. The revolution had started with a song about the village of brotherhood. That village never eventuated.

Diario de Noticias 28 August 1975, the second mass march 27 August: "The united left in the streets of Lisbon. 'Our revolution is in danger' says Vasco Goncalves to the crowd of more than 100,000 people"

"WE WANT GOUGH": AUSTRALIA NOVEMBER 1975

The Battler
17 December
1975

The Australian economy went from boom to bust in 1974, throwing the Whitlam Labor Government into disarray. In November of that year, aided by a few beers, I had predicted "a Liberal Government within twelve months". A year later it arrived right on time. Governor-General John Kerr dismissed the prime minister on 11 November 1975 and called new elections.

Janey and I returned from overseas in September and were immediately caught up in events, with numerous stoppages and rallies in defence of the government.

SWAG members turned up at demonstrations bearing placards with *The Battler* emblazoned across the top – the first time anyone did this on the Australian left. SWAG seemed to suddenly appear as a force, and even Gough Whitlam bought a *Battler*. We taped his 20 cent piece to our office wall, where it stayed until someone needed it for a phone call.

We were immersed in the erupting struggles. We were able to use our union connections to address a meeting at a large meatworks. We then got a bit carried away and the front page of *The Battler* on 11 November had the headline:

THIS IS HOW WE STOPPED FRASER

It was one of our more embarrassing moments. According to the SWAG Newsletter, "On Tuesday morning we had 800 *Battlers* ready to be sold at factories and shopping centres. By Tuesday night we had 800 unsellable *Battlers*. We produced 2,000 leaflets

THE Battler

PAPER OF THE SOCIALIST WORKERS' ACTION GROUP

Number 12, November 8, 1975.   10 cents

This is how we stopped Fraser

Melbourne
* Wharfies held a 24 hour stoppage, and marched to the ALP rally at City Square.
* Tug crews stopped work on Friday and again on Sunday night, pledging support for a general port stoppage.
* The Westernport industrial area stopped work for 24 hours, including refinery and maritime workers.
* More than 30 metal workshops for various lengths of time, including 1,400 Naval Dockyard workers.

Adelaide
* 1,000 workers from factories, building sites and factories rallied against Fraser.
* Workers from Islington Rail Workshops stopped work, and rail and metal unions encouraged workers to go to the rally.

Brisbane
* A meeting of 33 ALP-affiliated unions adopted a Meat Industry Union resolution recommending that the struggle should mobilise the full strength of unionists.

Perth
* Brewery workers stopped work and marched to a rally at the Town Hall.
* 2,000 railway workers stopped for the afternoon.
* The Fremantle waterfront stopped for 24 hours.

Hobart
* Waterside workers walked off the job to give Fraser a hostile reception.

Wollongong
* Port Kembla Maritime Unions Port Committee organised a 24 hour stoppage on Tuesday. Watchmen who worked during the stoppage will donate their pay to produce a leaflet about the government crisis.

Newcastle
* Waterfront unions, tug crews and PMG linesmen stopped work between 1 p.m. and 5 p.m. on October 30. This was followed by a rally and a march of 500 people.

Sydney
* Sydney waterfront workers stopped for 24 hours on Friday.

> ' Mr Fraser may make it impossible for a conservative party to govern in Australia with any measure of co-operation from the unions.'

THE NATIONAL TIMES NOVEMBER 3-8, 1975

Inside: More News on the Crisis

calling for a general strike, while the *Battler* staff worked 40 hours...producing a new *Battler*."

Three days later it was reissued with the headline "How we fought the coup". Over 700 copies were sold on that day and a reprint was immediately necessary.

After he was dismissed, Whitlam tried to reduce the matter to an electoral battle, but sections of the rank and file workers saw it differently and the stoppages escalated. These were the people we appealed to in *The Battler*.

The front page read:

> Whitlam had the votes, the
> Constitution and public support.
> Fraser had the bosses and the
> Governor-General ... he won.
> So much for democracy in parliament.
> Defend yourself with democracy
> on the job.

STRIKE TO STOP FRASER

We staged our biggest intervention on 14 November, when leftist unions called a mass rally in Melbourne's City Square (corner Swanston and Collins Streets). After listening to the likes of John Halfpenny, leader of the metal workers union and CP militant, doing

Part of a huge crowd of upwards of 30,000 which gathered in the Melbourne City Sq to protest with their presence at the dismissal of the elected Whitlam Government. participation represented the exercise of a democratic right. On December 13 they have the democratic right to follow through their protest at the ballot box. A furthe Square rally will be held tomorrow, Tuesday, December 2, at 12.30 pm. It wi sponsored by white collar industrial unions, and Mr Gough Whitlam, the elected F Minister, will be the main speaker.

their damnedest to keep feelings calm, perhaps 50,000 people marched up Collins Street to the Treasury Building, where the Labor Party politicians, the party hacks, the trade union officials and so on told everyone it was time to go home and "make your street a street for Labor". In other words, an electoral orientation.

But a lot of people didn't want to do this. Keen for further action, a breakaway march of 10,000 or so – a sizeable chunk of the crowd – followed our banners to Parliament House then back down Bourke Street to the centre of the city.

There we were - workers were following our banners. Meanwhile, at the front of the march a battle raged for control between Maoists, who wished to take the crowd to the US Consulate – a considerable distance away in St Kilda Road – and SWAG, who insisted on heading for the Stock Exchange. Each target had a political significance: the Maoists blamed the Kerr coup on the CIA and US imperialism, while we saw the struggle in class rather than national terms.

A combination of geography (the Stock Exchange was far closer), better organisation and superior political logic ensured victory for the IS tendency in this tussle.

But most of the crowd behind us were less ideological. We were leading the crowd down the hill at quite a pace, and were trying to get suitable chants going, such as calls for a general strike. But to no avail. The slogan that everybody wanted to hear was "We want Gough!" Gough Whitlam was the elected prime minister of Australia and people were angry that he had been dismissed. They wanted to chant "We want Gough". We, on the other hand, had been the most vociferous critics of Gough Whitlam and we definitely did *not* want Gough!

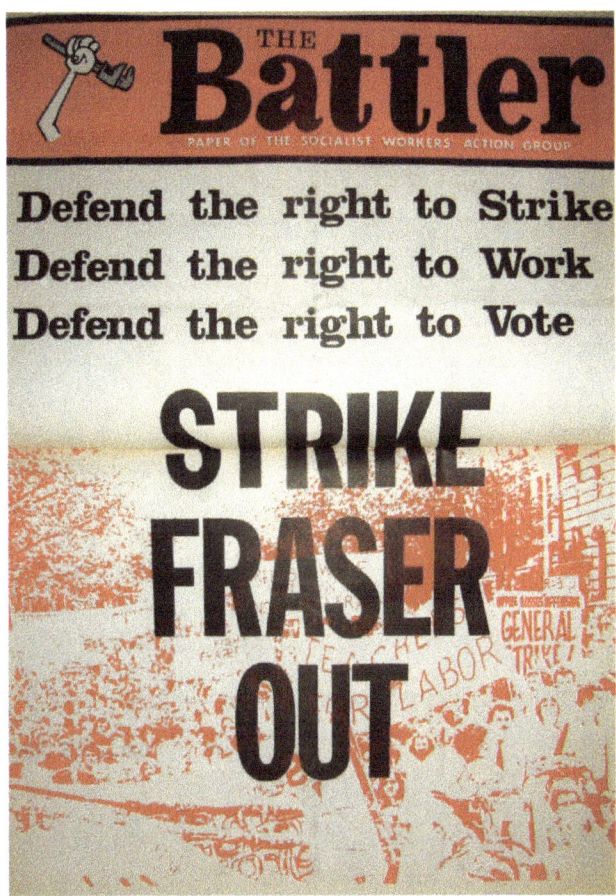

The Battler 19 November 1975; (opposite page) *Scope* 1 December 1975

But there was simply no choice. To hold the demonstration together, you had to join in this chant, build on this chant. I remember well how it tempered our exuberant mood to realise we could only hold the huge crowd together by taking up this slogan.

Phil Griffiths ended up leading the "We want Gough" chant, walking backwards at the front of the march, and shouting through a megaphone at the crowd following until he was red in the face. Some of the more sectarian elements of the far left came up to us and remonstrated "How can you say that?" Griff replied, ironically, "We're reformists!"

We were not reformists of course, but the crowd were, and we had to face that reality.

Another reality awaited us when we got to the Stock Exchange. The police had bolted the glass doors and arrayed themselves on the steps. They had the situation thoroughly under control, and our small forces could not charge the police lines. We tried to get everyone to sit down and listen to speeches, but they just would not sit down. I was working as a teacher at the time, and Janey remembers me getting them to sit down by calling out with what she calls my teacher's voice: "You there! Up the back! Sit down!"

The situation was an anti-climax. A young waterside worker voiced the frustration of many in the crowd. "You bring us all the way here," he told me angrily, "then you leave us flat!" I understood his reaction but could think of nothing to do.

After some jostling against police lines and a speech or two, the demonstration dispersed. Our accomplishment was to demonstrate that sizeable numbers of workers were looking for a militant lead. At the same time it was abundantly clear that groups like SWAG were too small to provide it. Meanwhile Melbourne's left union and ALP leaders, who actually were influential enough to lead a serious struggle, had shown their attitude by going home from Spring Street.

An internal document reviewing the events a few days later noted that we had not expected to find ourselves at the head of a march, so we were not organised to do the job. Amazingly, we had only one megaphone (at a demonstration of 40,000 people!). There was a comment that Griff should have given the megaphone to others more often so he could consult with people. It concluded:

> On Friday we bit off a little more than we could chew. We should have no regrets. We have considerably increased our standing on the left, gained in experience and confidence and learned lessons. Had we not intervened the march would have been leaderless, and would have disintegrated into a chaotic mass much earlier than it did... We followed Lenin's maxim: "audacity and more audacity". We should continue to do so.

Here is an article I wrote about the dismissal.

Conspiracy theories about dismissal obscure more important things

Red Flag
9 November 2015

Shocking revelations seem easy to get a hold of these days. Historian Jenny Hocking says leading conservative politicians were on the phone before the sacking of the Whitlam government. I'm aghast. Oh, and they had a special phone for affairs of state. Consider my gob thoroughly smacked.

Peter Barbour, who was director-general of ASIO from 1970 to 1975, tells us that Gough Whitlam gave the organisation oral rather than written instructions about talking to the CIA. This is sneaky, but working in the public service taught me that "avoiding leaving a paper trail" goes on all the time.

These mini-revelations will feed the ever-present conspiracy theories surrounding the dismissal. And that's a problem. Not that the conspiracies weren't present. But the chatter they arouse obscures more important things.

Let's travel back to a moment after the June 1975 Bass by-election. Whitlam was still in office, but Fraser was on the offensive and the economy was in trouble. Labor's primary vote dropped 17 percent and the Liberals won the seat 60-40 on a two-party preferred basis. After minerals and energy minister Rex Connor's resignation in October in the wake of the notorious "loans affair" coming to light, Fraser felt confident enough to block supply in the Senate and bring on a constitutional crisis.

At this point, according to Paul Kelly, "Fraser spoke with senior newspaper executives from at least two of Australia's three newspaper chains… Almost without exception the press supported Fraser's decision to force an election".

Meanwhile, the government met obstruction at every turn in trying to resolve the supply crisis. When Whitlam sought a half-Senate election, conservative state governments refused to cooperate. When he sought temporary finance from the banks, they refused to extend it, which in turn gave John Kerr a pretext for dismissing the government.

In October, Queensland governor

The Battler
17 December 1975

Colin Hannah and Robert Menzies joined the fray with a statement endorsing Fraser's actions.

There are elements of conspiracy in all this. But much more important was Fraser's ability to mobilise social forces. A mobilisation of social forces is not the same as a conspiracy, nor was there monolithic unity in the anti-Labor camp.

In fact, in the weeks before the dismissal, ruling class sentiment was fairly volatile. Shortly before Connor's resignation, the *Sydney Morning Herald* questioned Fraser's credibility: the opposition leader had begun hinting that "extraordinary or reprehensible" circumstances were not required to legitimise blocking supply, and the *Herald* suggested this new tack was itself "reprehensible".

After Connor's demise, the *Herald* changed its tune and declared "Fraser must act". Yet even then, he did not have an easy run. As Whitlam sought to tough out the supply crisis, the Liberal leader had a grim battle of his own keeping control of skittish backbenchers, while the breakaway Liberal Movement condemned his actions.

Sections of the media also remained nervous, the *Age* urging the Liberals to back down and the *Brisbane Courier-Mail* pleading repeatedly for compromise. W.J. Sharp, managing director of Jennings Industries, thought the political uncertainty bad for business confidence, telling the *National Times*:

"I am in favour of passing supply… I believe the story that the business community was urging the opposition to stop supply was a complete myth and ought to be scotched. If a survey of business people had been done one month ago, I am convinced that the vote would have been overwhelmingly against the Liberal Party doing what it did. My own recollection, from conversations in the last few weeks with dozens of businessmen, is that only one executive was in favour."

Among the media, there was a growing belief that Fraser had missed the boat. *The Bulletin* portrayed him as the "man in a muddle". The British *Economist* thought blocking supply had "begun to look like a smart tactic which went astray".

What overcame this ruling class fragmentation was not any of the conspiracies running at the time. It was Fraser's determined mobilisation. We're used to the idea that our side in the struggle must mobilise or face defeat – "If you don't fight you lose". But the other side faces the same imperative.

THE Battler
PAPER OF THE INTERNATIONAL SOCIALISTS

Number 14, December 17, 1975   10 cents

post-election special

You may have won the election Squire, but

THE FIGHT'S NOT OVER YET!

FRASER, PEACOCK, ANTHONY AND THE REST of the coalition were smirking on TV on election night. So were their media henchmen. You can tell Fraser thinks he's going to treat Australian workers like peasants on his country estate. The Melbourne Club will pour more champagne and count all the money they plan to make. The Stock Exchange will start cheering again.

The Libs still think they're born to rule. But we can wipe the sneering smile off Fraser's face.

The Labor Party has lost the elections. That doesn't mean that the Australian workers are beaten. Many people voted for Fraser out of desperation over unemployment and inflation. But Fraser's so-called solutions for the economy will be to force us to make more sacrifices. Only a minority of big business parasites voted for that. And when Fraser tries to do it, he can be stopped and beaten.

Labor's defeat was a disaster, but it isn't the end of the world. We have to learn the lessons from it, and go on to build a fighting workers' movement that can turn the tide against Fraser. This issue of the Battler is mostly devoted to learning those lessons and building that movement.

WIPE THE SMILE OFF FRASER'S FACE

INSIDE:
HOW TO FIGHT FRASER pages 4 and 5

I.S. IN AUSTRALIA: A NATIONAL ORGANISATION

Around the time of these big nationwide events, we changed our name to the International Socialists and moved to make the organisation more national. This was the third phase of our early years.

The change of name occurred at a rather grandly titled Regroupment Conference in December 1975, attended by about 40 people. Partly we just wanted a name change and this was a good opportunity. We wanted to use the name IS because of the association with the international tendency, but also it was time to move away from the unserious-sounding, cutesy name SWAG.

The regroupment was really a very modest unification with a small group from Tasmania (led by Rana Roy). But it was a start to spreading beyond Melbourne.

Griff used to say: "If you have two members in Melbourne, keep one there and send the other one to Sydney." In this spirit, Janey and I and a couple of other comrades

Tom and Diane Fieldes, 1980; (opposite page) *The Batter* 17 December 1975

moved to Sydney in early 1976. We already had good contacts there, and we quickly established a functional branch. This positioned us to relate to people we were attracting in other parts of Australia.

In Canberra David Lockwood, Ian Jordan and Tony Roberts joined quickly, with Diane Fieldes following a little later. In Brisbane Carole Ferrier and Graham Grassie established a branch in 1976. John Minns and Ian Rintoul, previously members of the anarchist-oriented Self-Management Group, joined soon afterwards, as did Judy McVey.

Part of the growth in Brisbane also came from the Mt Isa branch of the Communist Party. Its leader, John Boyd, had done a national speaking tour to build trade union support for the Movement Against Uranium Mining. He discovered that in the major cities, the left group most committed to this was the IS. He and his CP comrades also realised that while they had found their way to revolutionary politics, the party they belonged to was moving the other way. A number of them joined us in 1978.

I.S. in Australia: a national organisation

For a short time we had a branch in Wollongong, where there was a working class network that was more left wing than the Communists – real militant Labor Left. Through George Petersen (father of IS member Eric Petersen), who was a Labor MP and a leading figure in this milieu, we were able to meet many people. We learnt a lot about how to relate to working class militants.

Although still modest and still with internal tensions, within a couple of years after the establishment of the International Socialists, we had a national organisation. In spite of all the limitations, I can't emphasise enough what it meant to grow from a group of a dozen people in Melbourne to a national organisation with real branches in Sydney, Brisbane, Canberra and a small one also in Adelaide. Having a national organisation – that small presence in the major cities – changed the way we thought about ourselves.

By the time of the 1977 conference, we had a membership of around 70, which rose to about 100 by 1980. Organisers wore a groove in the map along the route from Brisbane to Sydney and Canberra, and on to Melbourne and Adelaide, sometimes hitching, sometimes travelling by overnight train. We would

arrive in a town, lead discussions, join in whatever demonstrations were happening, and then we rode over the horizon.

Our branches flourished through this period due to our ability to latch on to opportunities. The best example is probably Brisbane. No sooner was the branch established than arch right wing Premier Joh Bjelke-Petersen shook up the whole political environment in Queensland by banning street marches.

The subsequent civil liberties movement produced a political ferment. John Minns wrote that "the small Brisbane left suddenly found itself in organising meetings

Clockwise from left: Carole Ferrier; John Minns; Queensland anti-uranium picket of Hamilton wharf 1978, Tony Bloodworth and Sandra Bloodworth; (below) Tony Bloodworth with "U", Vicky Spiteri with "M"

Tom giving a talk for the Seattle ISO (US), January 1978. *Socialist Worker* (US) February 1978

AUSTRALIAN SOCIALIST IN SEATTLE

SEATTLE, WA—On Tuesday, January 17, the Seattle branch of the ISO and the Crabshell Alliance, a local anti-nuclear power group co-sponsored a meeting on the Australian anti-uranium movement. 50 people attended.

Paul Finley explained the basic goals of the Crabshell Alliance in the Washington area.

Tom O'Lincoln, a leader of the Australian International Socialists, a fraternal group of the ISO, and a participant in the anti-uranium mining struggle, gave a history of that movement.

LABOR

O'Lincoln described the labor movement's involvement in the movement including their refusal to load or remove uranium going in or out of Australia.

The anti-nuclear movement in Australia is remarkable for a number of reasons. The first is that there are no nuclear power plants in the entire country. Furthermore,

Tom O'Lincoln

the workers who refuse to load the uranium are attempting to prevent other countries from using it.

O'Lincoln ended his talk by stressing the importance of building an international movement against the spread of nuclear power.

O'Lincoln also spoke to a meeting of anti-nuclear power activists in Portland.

of hundreds which went on until the middle of the night, and it was able to mobilise thousands of people – all in the course of a few weeks." The young IS branch did this so well that Bjelke-Petersen warned specifically against the "well-known Communist Graeme Grassie" and his comrade Carole Ferrier, "an extremist, revolutionary type of individual and a well-known member of the International Socialists".

A leading activist in the civil liberties campaign and the Movement Against Uranium Mining (MAUM) was Sandra Bloodworth, and this is when we first encountered her. Sandra was not a typical "student type" activist; she had been a bank teller, and was married with children. This was her first exposure to political activism, and with major talents as a speaker and in other ways, she moved into leadership rapidly. After she moved to Melbourne in 1978 she joined the IS, a real coup for our little group.

During this period of growth in the late 1970s however we also made mistakes.

Janey and I had visited the UK in July 1975 and encountered the British International Socialists for the first time. After our stay in Lisbon in August we went to Detroit, the headquarters of the American IS, where there were now some people we had known in Berkeley, including Joel Geier.

Both the American IS and the British IS had developed a strategic orientation of a turn to the industrial working class. But the American group implemented this in a different way. They argued: "the revolution is going to happen quickly, we need to get a base in the working class as fast as we can". The strategy, known as industrialisation, cut corners and meant middle class students going work in factories. We were very impressed with their successes in engaging with militant workers and their strategy seemed at the time very exciting to us.

Janey and I took this idea back to Australia, where we proposed the implementation of industrialisation here, based on the argument that the group "needs to make the transition to being a workers' organisation as quickly as possible". The proposal was presented rather grandly as "the first step to becoming a workers' combat organisation". The other members said, "Well why don't you lead the charge and go work in some factory yourself?" A few of us did actually attempt to do this, to the extent of working in blue collar jobs for a time. I worked in a sheet metal factory for a couple of months and Janey spent eight months in a factory in Sydney where she was a shop steward in the metal workers' union.

But industrialisation as a strategy to achieve a base in the working class was never going to work. The idea that it could is the result of impatience. It assumes ex-students can go in and substitute themselves for the activity of the working class itself. In practice, they generally don't fit in well in a blue collar environment. When I worked as a sheet metal worker, it wasn't long before my fellow workers started asking where I went to university. So you try anxiously to fit in, which puts you under conservatising pressures. "Industrialised" ex-students are tempted to accommodate to majority attitudes on the job. It also breeds authoritarianism – because despite disclaimers, few members wanted to work in factories. Although we tried moral pressure very few people did actually get factory jobs.

The fortnightly paper we had started around the same time lasted a bit longer. This was the first of several attempts to get a fortnightly off the ground without a strong financial base and it resulted in our political leadership being unduly tied up with fund-raising. We ran a typesetting business as way of financing the paper, or at least that was the idea, but it lost money and we spent hours agonising about it. Looking back, though, our ability to grow had little to do with our publication schedule.

This is not the place for a detailed

Leaflet for gay demonstration 4 November 1978

account of these early years and I have only touched on a few highlights. For anyone who is interested in knowing more there are two sources. One is the "unofficial" history written by Phil Ilton. Although it reflects Phil's own views when written in 1978, when he was no longer himself a member, it is a very useful summary of events. Phil noted in his closing paragraph, "Big oaks from little acorns grow". Commenting on this in the preface to his history which we published in pamphlet form in 1984, I wrote:

> And while the IS is at best a somewhat large acorn, rather than being an oak, it is true that the roots of our present national organisation lie in the struggle to build a much smaller group in one city in the early seventies.

I went on to relate the transformations we had just gone through to our earlier history:

> The perspectives and policies of SWAG on a number of questions were somewhat different than those of the IS today. For example, we are considerably more critical today of the idea of separate women's organising, and we now stand firmly on the state capitalist analysis of the eastern bloc states. Nevertheless the underlying political continuity is impressive. And it has been the basics of IS politics, often summed up in the phrase "revolutionary socialism from below", which have allowed us to survive and grow in difficult times, while so much of the left has fallen into confusion and decline. These basics were established in SWAG over several years of political struggle.

The other source is the account I wrote of the group's history in 1992, *Marching Down Marx Street*. It gives some of the events of the period in more detail than I've included in these memoirs.

Growing understanding of Marxism

During this period my understanding of Marxism was developing, both through reading and by encounters with leading Marxists in our tendency. Having been in the American IS, I might have been expected to stick with Shachtmanism but in fact I drifted steadily into the British IS's theoretical orbit. During our visit to Britain in 1975, Janey and I stayed with Ian Birchall and Nora Carlin, and we met several other leaders of the British IS, including Tony Cliff.

A key influence on me was the writings of Nigel Harris. More so than Cliff, whose work could be formulaic, Harris built his work around a sense of the dynamic character of capitalism. Eventually he abandoned key aspects of IS politics, but his early analyses were very valuable for me.

This was embodied in a number of books and essays which can only be called brilliant, including the seminal book *Beliefs in Society*, on the origins of Stalinism, Marxism's journey east, and a sustained and ferocious critique of third worldism. "Isn't he wonderfully articulate?" grumbled a rival paper seller one Melbourne day.

In 1976, Harris was the first leading British member to visit Australia. As well as his value to us as a public speaker, Nigel also posed an organisational challenge to our small group. Nigel argued against the policy of industrialisation and convinced us that it was substitutionist.

When I came to Australia, I had set out to educate the people of another land in Shachtmanism, with little success. It now seemed to be a purely American phenomenon. Nobody from the British group ever abandoned "Cliffism" to become an Australian Shachtmanite.

A phrase Nigel Harris often used had a big impact on me: "the rhythm of revolt". I loved that phrase and used it often. Nigel based it on a materialist analysis and he argued powerfully. If you were on the receiving end of one of his harangues, you certainly knew it.

In the late 1970s and early 1980s, I was also reading in a serious way. I was travelling a lot and when doing that I was reading Mandel's *Marxist Economic Theory* as preparation for reading *Capital*. If I had to do this again, I'd do it the other way around, Marx first then Mandel.

The two standout works of Marx are *Capital* and the *Communist Manifesto*. They were written for different levels, in different atmospheres, under different conditions. The *Manifesto* was written in the flow-on from the revolutions in Europe, which is certainly not the case for *Capital*.

Capital is unique in its explanation of how the world works, and how capitalism works. Once you've read *Capital*, nothing else is the same. While it is indispensable reading in economics, philosophy or sociology, the greatness of *Capital* lies mainly in another dimension: apart perhaps from the *Communist Manifesto*, it's the greatest argument ever written to fight for a better world.

Capital enriched my thinking in two fundamental ways: on capital, and on dialectics. Both of these are about how the world works: getting down to the bottom of the cesspool, finding the mechanisms that make it happen. What you discover is that for almost every situation that you're in – in a non-dogmatic way – there is a way out. Marx's *Capital* gave me the ability to grasp the dynamic of capitalism.

I read the whole thing through twice and even today often something prompts me to go and look at *Capital* again.

After reading *Capital*, I tackled the harder but equally important question of the dialectic, particularly through Hegel's *Logic*. Having read the first hundred pages I gave up: it was too hard. But I did go on to read the whole of the *Phenomenology of Mind*. The dynamic of what Hegel was trying to do, and why it has so much to do with capitalism, are things I have put into talks that I've given to help give people a feel for the ideas. For most people it's too hard to get it directly out of Hegel partly because it's in German. For us the really important thing is applying Hegel's *Logic* and Marx's *Capital* to different situations as we encounter them. Reading those works, and trying to apply them over the years, gave me more confidence in my abilities.

Rank and file activity

Central to our concept of the paper was to involve worker militants in selling and writing for it, aiming to develop a network and then recruit from it. We wanted to link the paper closely to the class struggle and the militants. In one sense, this was highly successful. Quite a few militants sold it on the job.

In another sense the whole thing was smoke and mirrors. Looking casually at the paper, it was bursting with workers' struggles. We presented them well and workers liked it, but they also sensed it wasn't entirely real. They would sell it, but would seldom join the organisation behind it.

However, there really was a layer of rebellious workers in industry, and sometimes they did challenge the union bureaucracy. We were right to throw ourselves into their struggles.

This orientation informed our work right through the 1970s.

One way to engage with this layer was through strike support work, which gave us confidence and coherence. The group involved itself in a printers' strike at the Melbourne *Herald* in 1975. Most of our members joined the picket, and we distributed a leaflet about it in Housing Commission (public housing) areas where we sold our new paper. In the aftermath, a shop steward at the *Herald* was selling 40-plus copies of *The Battler* on the job.

During a Victorian state-wide meatworkers' strike in 1975, some members spent whole nights on the picket, and Griff built a close relationship with the striking workers. In 1978 the Melbourne members mobilised to support the workers

Sit-in of Sanyo workers in Wodonga, Victoria 1978; *International Socialist* No10 August 1980

at Sanyo in Wodonga, who had occupied their factory to defend their jobs. In 1979, 55 workers at the Union Carbide petrochemical plant in Altona in Melbourne's west embarked on Australia's longest unbroken factory occupation. IS members produced a poster and leaflet in an effort to build support for the sit-in, which lasted 51 days.

We were learning to relate to workers in struggle. These experiences gave greater substance to our ideas about building a rank and file movement in industry, which we had taken from the British and American IS.

Unfortunately our orientation also bred illusions which caused problems in the subsequent period. Because its main stock in trade was ideas and it could seldom deliver concrete gains in struggle, a group as small as ours needed to orient first and foremost to the campuses, where the interest in ideas for their own sake was highest. Interventions in the working class were really a means to demonstrate the relevance of those ideas to students and the general left. But instead we allowed our student work to run down after the Monash occupation, while devoting endless hours to attempts to get a toehold in industry and working class neighbourhoods.

Union activist: Teacher Action

The area where we were able to engage in the class struggle directly was among white collar workers, because we had members there. Through our rank and file activity we gained experience that continues to stand us in good stead.

One such area was teachers. I was personally involved between 1972 and 1974, when I was a teacher at Maribyrnong High in Melbourne's western suburbs. This school had a reputation for militancy and being troublesome: people would smile knowingly when I told them I was at Maribyrnong. Perhaps it was because a strike the previous year had become confrontational, with the head of the union branch throwing a punch at the principal.

I became a member of the Victorian Secondary Teachers Association (VSTA) and immediately set up a rank and file group with some others, namely Roger Holdsworth and Phil Noyce, both independents and Jim McIlroy, a member of the Socialist Youth Alliance. Shortly afterwards Graeme Smith, an IS member, also joined. Tess Lee Ack was drawn into that group in a limited way, as she was still a student.

We were a small group of teachers who had met through the left, and we put out a publication called *Teacher Action*. Although it covered industrial issues and topics like how to win strikes, this was more from theory than experience and was rather long-winded. There was a strong argument along the lines of needing to democratise the union. We also campaigned for Helen Garner who was sacked for saying "unseemly

Secondary teachers' strike in Victoria 1974. The Teacher Action banner can be seen in both photos with the slogan "Teachers' rights, Teacher Action"

things" in the classroom.

Our main achievement was the introduction of ideas, the most important of which was the idea of rank and file organising. Another was the argument that ex-students and parents were natural allies for teachers in their struggles, which was a particular favourite of Roger's.

I spoke at a regional mass meeting within a couple of weeks of the formation of *Teacher Action*. It was the first time I ever spoke at such a meeting as a worker in a particular industry. I was described by somebody who saw me as looking "angry". In reality I was just nervous. Anyhow, I got lots of applause.

Although we were a small group of committed socialists working within a large union organisation, *Teacher Action* had real roots among rank and file teachers. There were layers of activists from those on the far left through to the very moderate, which included some union officials. There were also a lot of new teachers from the US, who had been recruited to address Victoria's teacher shortage. Initially they were astonished at how radical Australian teachers were, but in the end some of them began to be influenced and moved left. Perhaps their experience around the anti-Vietnam War issue was a factor.

Sometimes a hard-core rank and file group can commit the error of substituting itself for real grassroots militants. But in the early 1970s, we were dealing with genuine militants beyond our ranks and constant strikes and threats of strikes was the general atmosphere of the times. In the end, we were able to build a network beyond our core which was significant.

How radical the atmosphere was is clear when you consider that the VSTA leadership decided on a policy of open admission to universities, arguing that anyone should be allowed to enrol. If resources were limited, they proposed universities should select students by ballot, which would level out class backgrounds. This was a very daring proposal – controversial even among us – and an opposition faction within the union killed it fairly quickly, but in the meantime it gave us opportunities. I spoke at Monash as a union representative, and the RevComms at Monash established an Assessment Action Group to campaign for open admissions and an end to competitive assessment.

Although our particular grouping

lasted only a couple of years, *Teacher Action* set a tradition within the VSTA and other groups followed. The year 1981 again saw a ferment in the schools because the teachers' union leadership had allowed forcible transfer of teachers from one school to another. A group called Teacher Solidarity (after the Polish workers' rebellion) was formed and got 30 to 40 percent of the vote at mass meetings.

At the end of 1975, I taught for three months at Bentleigh High, where I had a couple of experiences which were not very political but illuminating to me personally. The students had seen me arriving at school every day in a car with a female teacher, who was just giving me a lift; but they reckoned they had the whole thing figured out. I had a very brightly coloured parka which I wore to a gay demonstration one day and there I was, very recognisable on TV. Colour TV had just come to Australia then and that parka was very conspicuous. When I went back to school the students asked me curiously, "Are you a poofter Mr O'Lincoln?"

They were surprised that I had been at a gay demo, but they took it in their stride.

IS members were very active in a network of action groups in the Administrative and Clerical Officers Association (ACOA) in the Commonwealth Public Service. The first of these was the ACOA Reform Group (ARG) set up in in Victoria in 1976, which still had an orientation to the union bureaucracy. Later rank and file public service militants in a number of states organised around a paper called *Grey Collar*.

During a 1981 dispute in the Department of Social Security (DSS), the ACOA had placed work bans and demanded extra staff. The government stood workers down and then NSW members walked off the job. The *Grey Collar* group agitated successfully for a union-wide stop-

1. Mick Segreto
2. Verity Burgmann
3. Pam Townshend
4. Martin Hirst
5. Dave Shaw
6. Brad Bowden
7. Tom Freeman
8. Mick Armstrong

Clockwise from top: Sydney branch at Kempsey summer camp, NSW early 1978, from Verity Burgmann's ASIO file; Canberra branch 1977 (left to right) Rick Kuhn, Verity Burgmann, Dave Shaw, Diane Fieldes; Kempsey (left to right) Mick Segreto, Phil Lee, Dave Shaw, Graeme Grassie, Mick Armstrong, Pam Townshend, Albert Tierney, Brad Bowden, Andrew Milner, Martin Hirst. Photos courtesy of Verity Burgmann

work meeting, and over a thousand unionists turned out in pouring rain. During the dispute, the *Grey Collar* group attracted 60 public servants to a rank and file conference, where the IS explained its strategy to build a rank and file movement.

We also had successful rank and file activity in the Victorian Public Service Association (VPSA). The VPSA Reform Group (VRG) began life as an anti-uranium mining group for VPSA members in 1978, after an attempt to set up a general rank and file group was unsuccessful. VRG was able to build an impressive base at the office-floor level; eventually IS member Jeff Soar and his associates got 47 percent of the vote in a union election at the height of their activity.

Phil Griffiths meanwhile had established himself in the insurance industry, and he began agitating for an equal pay campaign which eventually gripped the industry. The story is told in *Rebel Women*, the book I edited with Sandra Bloodworth.

Rick Kuhn makes an important point about this white collar activity:

> It demonstrated that the form of organisation appropriate for socialists' activity in other unions – the "rank and file strategy" – was also applicable there. Further it indicated that the whole working class, not just blue collar workers, are capable of shaping their own futures in a militant way and potentially in a socialist direction.[13]

One blue collar area where we had direct connections was among Sydney building workers. The NSW branch of the Builders Labourers Federation under Communist Party member Jack Mundey was famous in the early 1970s for the establishment of green bans. They also supported many other political campaigns such as Aboriginal rights and anti-war movements. Dave Shaw, a builders' labourer, joined the IS in Canberra in 1977. Although he was tertiary-educated and from a middle class background, Dave was comfortable in a working class environment, and developed into a real working class fighter. He became a rigger in Sydney and a significant figure in BLs for Democratic Control, a network of militants.

After the federal BLF leadership destroyed the NSW branch in 1974, safety on building sites deteriorated. Dave Shaw fell to his death in 1978 at the age of 22. Given the atmosphere of intense conflict at the time, there was speculation as to whether the fall was accidental.

IS intervention in the 1976 defend Medibank campaign

Extract from *Marching Down Marx Street*

The rank and file perspective also guided our intervention in the 1976 union campaign to defend the Medibank health insurance scheme, which the Fraser Government had set out to destroy. When the ALP proved a totally ineffectual opposition, it fell to the unions to fight back.

It was the workers of the NSW South Coast who made the first important move. This was a militant area. Delegates voted by 426 to 17 for a 24-hour stoppage. We were still new to NSW, but we put out a very presentable four-page publication and established good links with some militants. On 7 June some 40,000 workers throughout the district struck for the day. Around the same time, a meeting of about 30 Victorian left unions prodded the Victorian Trades Hall Council (THC) to make plans for a four-hour strike, to be presented at a delegates' meeting.

Two days later, 1500 shop stewards and job delegates packed Melbourne's Dallas Brooks Hall. Under these circumstances the four-hour strike proposal put forward by Trades Hall appeared utterly inadequate to a large section of the meeting, yet the left union officials continued to back it. A Communist Party leaflet distributed to arriving delegates called on them to "vote for action", but specified none. It seemed the four-hour proposal might triumph by default...but there was one alternative. A leaflet signed by a collection of shop stewards and circulated by the International Socialists demanded a 24-hour stoppage, and called for weekly stoppages in every State as a move towards generalised national strike action.

When Max Costello, an IS member and Technical Teachers' delegate, moved the proposal he won an overwhelming endorsement. "The mood was very angry," Max later told me. "Whoever got up and moved for stronger action, it was going to get carried." The delegates returned to work looking forward to the 24-hour strike. But there was alarm in the workplaces the next day, when they learned that the Trades Hall Executive was deadlocked eight to eight on whether to proceed with it. Two days later the alarm gave way to outrage after the full Council voted to stick to the original four-hour proposal, with mass meetings of strikers to be held at Festival Hall and suburban venues.

The militants were beside themselves. The IS rushed out leaflets overnight to the doorsteps of key shop stewards – a network we had established through our "workers' paper" project. Partly because of this agitation, telephone calls began to pour into union offices. By the time the stoppage took place on 16 June, the left union leaders had recognised that they risked being outbid by the tiny forces of the revolutionary left. They made an abrupt left turn.

Whereas at the Dallas Brooks Hall meeting, Communist Party union leader John Halfpenny had lined up with the right, now he appeared before 6000 angry strikers at Festival Hall as the vengeful champion of the militants, taking the floor to demand the 24-hour stoppage go ahead. Max Costello, moving a slightly different proposal, was heard respectfully, but he had suddenly become irrelevant. There was still plenty of rank and file anger though: at one stage a nurse snatched the microphone from Halfpenny's hand to address the crowd.

Seeing the strong rank and file response in Victoria, some key federal unions announced their own plans for a national stoppage. However by this stage, a combination of bureaucratic inertia and clever manoeuvring by ACTU Secretary Bob Hawke was beginning to turn the tide against the militants at the national level. The national strike was a token effort and the strike wave subsided.

Clockwise from top: Tom with representative of Palestinian women's organisation; woman waving Palestinian flag in demonstration during the general strike; Tom, Mick and Janey with Fatih Arafat, head of Palestinian Red Crescent in Beirut; Tom and Mick with participants in demonstration during the general strike; (opposite page) Beirut January 1980. Left to right: Mick, representative of Popular Front, Janey, Tom

REFUGEE CAMPS AND SCRABBLE: LEBANON AND PALESTINE 1980

Janey Stone, Mick Armstrong and I went to Lebanon in 1980. It was January, during the northern winter. The civil war between the right wing (Maronite Christians) and the left wing (Palestinian forces allied with pan-Arabic and Muslim groupings) had been going on since 1975. The Syrian army entered the country and stabilised the situation in 1976, and the Israelis gained control of a strip of land along the border in 1978. At the time we visited, the country was effectively divided, with southern Lebanon and western Beirut under the control of the PLO and the Lebanese left. Eastern Beirut was controlled by the Christian militias, with the boundary known as the Green Line.

On arriving in West Beirut, we were struck by the ruined buildings, garbage dumps and shanty towns. Water and electricity supplies continually broke down. The refugee camps held thousands of Palestinians expelled from Israel in the various wars since 1948. Although some "camps" (more like whole city blocks) had been there for decades, the Lebanese authorities deemed them "temporary" settlements and compelled them to build open sewers. In winter, these urban ghetto-like areas were a sea of mud. Rats grew fat on the rubbish heaps, and flies and mosquitoes spread periodic epidemics.

Some Lebanese communists in Sydney had arranged contacts for us with Beirut representatives of the Union of Lebanese Communists (not the official Moscow aligned party), with whom we had interesting discussions. One of them took us to the cinema, to our surprise carefully stowing a gun. We couldn't see why that would be necessary. But standing in the cinema foyer we understood: we could hear an exchange of gunfire in the street outside.

Only a couple of days after our arrival a general strike shut down most of Lebanon in protest at the "normalisation" of relations between Egypt and Israel. Mick described the scene in an article in the *Battler*:

> In West Beirut, the area dominated by the Palestinians and the Lebanese left forces, not only was industry shut down by the general strike, but as well, most shops were closed and the normally numerous taxis were off the roads. Armed Palestinians and leftists marched to Beirut's Arab University for a rally to denounce the normalisation. We joined the demonstration there.

By 11 o'clock the street outside the university courtyard was a sea of demonstrators, many of them waving Kalashnikovs (sub-machine guns). But there were also many small children carrying flags and placards. An old woman danced to the rhythm of the chanting. Someone handed her a Kalashnikov and she flourished it above her head as she danced. The demonstrators were greeted at the University by leading Palestinian and leftist leaders, including Yasser Arafat of Fatah and George Habash of the Popular Front for the Liberation of Palestine.[14]

Our contacts introduced us to the PLO office in Beirut, which operated as a sort of radical tourist office, running tours, a cafeteria and even providing us with a flat. Each day the PLO office provided a guide and driver and we visited many organisations and individuals in Beirut.

The representatives of the Popular Front for the Liberation of Palestine (PFLP) whom we met predicted that another Israeli invasion of Lebanon supported by their Lebanese Phalangist allies (the right wing party supported by Lebanese Christians) would occur before the end of the year. The timing was not accurate, but the event did occur two years later in 1982.

At the Palestinian Red Crescent office, we met Fathi Arafat, founder and head of the organisation, who was Yasser Arafat's brother and his spitting image. Fathi was very friendly and welcoming to us. We talked about the refugee camps. He told us that it was not possible to make substantial changes in their conditions, so the Red Crescent was restricted to educating families in household cleanliness and limited preventative measures. In relation to hospitals, Fatih said, "Our problem is how to develop a medical plan for such a scattered people. It is even harder because our lives are unstable. We wait for air raids, we wait to see if we will be expelled."

The director of the Nursing School, Mustafa Jamaa, told us,

> We can't count the number of times the Israelis have attacked the hospitals. They do it deliberately. That is why our operating theatres are underground… They want us to kneel, but we will never kneel.

Upon leaving the Red Crescent office we encountered Yasser Arafat himself, but it was an opportunity foregone. We came down in the lift, and as the lift door opened, there he was standing right in front of us and looking right at us! A photo opportunity – but we felt too shy. Janey thought "I don't want to be crass" … and for nearly 40 years she has wished she had been crass!

The Union of Palestinian Women were quite surprised that we asked to meet a representative. It seems they were rated by many visitors as not very interesting, but for us the role of women in the struggle was fundamental.

One day the PLO took us on a tour to places outside the city, including the Rashidiye Palestinian refugee camp in southern Lebanon, the town of Damour and the old crusader fortress of Beaufort, at the time occupied by the Palestinians. This was a unique opportunity to see and meet many people engaged in the struggle. We were particularly moved by our exposure to the refugees, and sitting with the fighters in Beaufort was an experience never to be forgotten.

A *Time* magazine journalist followed us around as we did the tour. Afterwards he went off to file his story, which appeared with some nice photographs. The story covered the same topics as ours, but we felt different as supporters.

Here is the article I wrote for *The Battler* on our visit to Lebanon.

The people behind a thirty year struggle

***The Battler*, 29 March 1980 (slightly edited)**

We have been in Beirut for only three days when there is a general strike. Israel and Egypt are normalising relations, and the PLO officials promise us the masses will "show their fury". We are on the spot early to see the first contingents arrive for the mass rally. There are plenty of guns. In a city full of armed militias, this is the biggest show of force we've seen.

Behind the armed fighters come the masses: contingents of workers, men and women, groups of children holding banners. Every contingent is led by someone with a loud hailer, perched on the shoulders of the comrades. The chanting is deafening. An old woman is dancing to the rhythm of the chants. Someone hands her a machine gun, and she flourishes it above her head as she dances.

...

Not long after the general strike we visit the Southern town of Damour. Many survivors of the terrible battles of Tel Al Zataar live here. Em Moussa, mother of seven, invites us into her home. On the wall is a photo of her son, who died at Tel Al Zataar. Three other children were injured. Em Moussa has seen tragedy enough, but she says, "We will keep fighting to the last. Even if our last child is killed, we will sacrifice for our struggle. I tell my daughters, 'You are becoming fighters to liberate our people'."

We ask her daughter, Samira, aged nine, what she wants to grow up to be. "I'll become a fighter, to fight Zionism and return to Palestine," she replies. It might only be childish enthusiasm. But Samira reveals she has been training with guns since she was six.

...

It is only a short distance to the southern front. We walk through the mud of Rashidiye refugee camp, which is continually harassed by Israeli ships and planes. We see the Christian quarter of Tyre, where residents point out what has been done to their houses by Israeli random shelling.

About noon we find ourselves in the ancient crusader castle of Beaufort, now occupied by the "Joint Forces" of the PLO and the Lebanese left. Across the river is a fascist enclave. Its commander, Saad Haddad, has virtually annexed it to Israel. We can see his

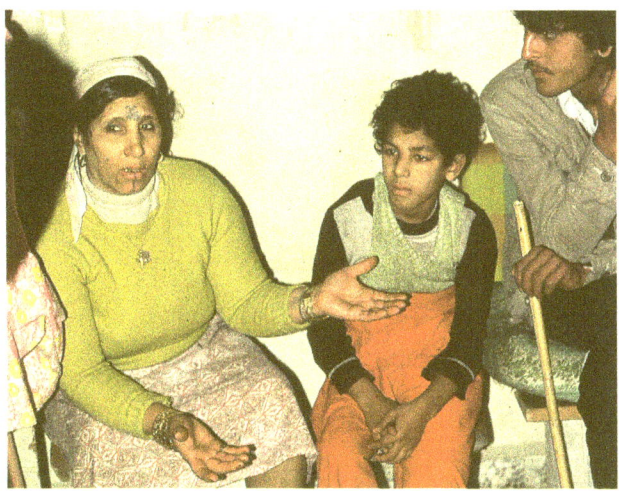

Samira with her brother; Em Moussa

towns with the naked eye. We can also see the northern tip of Israel. Between these three fires sits a forlorn looking United Nations outpost.

There is shelling here every day. The day after our visit, a direct hit knocks out all power in nearby Nabatiye. But all we see is a quiet sunny afternoon. Our hosts are Fatah combat troops. We drink sweet black tea with them in a crusader vault. They call it "Whiskey-Fatah", as PLO fighters are not allowed to drink alcohol. These men radiate the quiet confidence of combat veterans. The Israelis have tried and failed eight times to take this hill.

…

Back in Beirut, we end our visit by interviewing Jehan Helou, a leader of the Union of Palestinian Women.

"The Palestinian woman has always been part of the struggle," she says, "though she faces a three-fold burden – national, class and sex oppression. We have to overcome backward attitudes and raise consciousness. We teach women their potential is unlimited. You can be a fantastic mother and a fantastic freedom fighter at the same time."

Jehan is ready with the proof. "I have seen with my own eyes how in 1969 the Lebanese army tried to enter our camps. The women stood in front of the tanks and said, you will never enter except over our dead bodies. And the tanks stayed out.

"Women fought and died at Tel Al Zataar. One was a wireless operator, and had to fight her way in to replace a wounded radio man. They fought in the militias in Jordan and Lebanon. In Palestine the Israelis have imprisoned dozens of our women for military and other actions."

We think of little Samira, nine years old and learning to shoot. And we remember James Connolly's words: "The rising of the women is the rising of the race".

General strike in Beirut January 1980. Palestinian leaders acknowledge the crowd. From second left: Yasser Arafat (Fateh), Nayef Hawatmeh (Democratic Front), George Habash (Popular Front); Rashidiye refugee camp Southern Lebanon; Bir Zeit University, Ramallah, occupied West Bank

Nazareth: dark reports from the holy city

From Lebanon we went to Syria. I wrote in a postcard to my parents, which now seems very ironic, that we were " hopefully beyond the reach of any gunfire". At the border we had our bags searched four times. We visited Homs where we had contacts. A sharp, cold wind battered the plains behind the town, which has now been bombed almost out of existence. After a tourist visit to Jordan, we crossed the Allenby Bridge into Israel. The Arabs on our transit bus were taken off to be processed separately. Janey, Mick and I went through a relatively normal border crossing search, and were treated very politely by the Israeli border guards. Their search was very detailed, including squeezing our tubes of toothpaste, but they found nothing suspicious – we had posted all our Lebanese political material home. A travel Scrabble set raised the most interest. The guard thought it was a very good educational game.

In a postcard to my parents I wrote: "There were intensive security checks but actually it didn't take all that long. And this while Jordan and Israel are technically at war!"

Once in Israel, we linked up with political activists, attending a meeting of the Israeli Socialist Organisation, known by the name of their magazine *Matzpen*, and also visited Bir Zeit University, near Ramallah on the occupied West Bank, which is a centre of Palestinian activism.

On a previous visit in 1975 Janey and I had stayed with relatives living in Nazareth. Years later I was reminded of this and wrote the following.

Sabra refugee camp Beirut

Report from Nazareth[15]

In the flood of Middle East war reports, one phrase caught my eye. A Hezbollah rocket had reached "the holy city of Nazareth".

We're not supposed to ponder this too much, I suppose. They want us to think briefly of Jesus, curse perfidious Arabs and move on. But for me it brought back memories. I've met a few Nazarenes in my time, under two sets of very different circumstances.

One occasion was in a Beirut refugee camp. These were Palestinians driven from their Nazareth homes by the Zionists in 1948, and still languishing in exile decades later. Life was grim, but they welcomed us with smiles and tea, and spoke hopefully of their Palestinian revolution. Their families are probably still in those camps today, as Israeli bombers fly mercilessly overhead.

The other time was in Nazareth itself, where I met Jewish Israelis. They came from Australia and Russia. The Australians had stashes of vegemite, posted from Melbourne. The Russians had all set up stalls at the base of their high rise flats, offering themselves as watchmakers. How they could all make a living was a mystery. But they were a lot better off than people in the Beirut camps.

Here is one of those simple, screaming obscenities amidst the complexities of the Middle East conflict. If you're Jewish and born in Melbourne or Moscow, you have the right to go to Israel. But Arab refugees born in Nazareth are banned from their home town, because Israel's core ideology – Zionism – embodies a cancerous racism.

Cancer spreads. In 1967 Israel seized the West Bank and Sinai. Then Jewish settlements began to appear throughout the occupied territories. The Palestinians fought back with brave but outgunned militias; driven out of Jordan, they regrouped in Lebanon.

Not long after my visit to Beirut, Israel invaded Lebanon. The initial rationale was to clear a zone in the south, to stop radical militias threatening Israel's security. But once the tanks began to roll, the murderous onslaught continued on to Beirut. In the aftermath, Ariel Sharon gave the green light for massacres in the refugee camps.

Refugee camps and Scrabble

I.S. IN AUSTRALIA: THE 1980s

The years 1975 to 1983 were dominated politically by the prime ministership of Malcolm Fraser, hated by all on the left and in the workers' movement because of his role in the dismissal of Whitlam. To set the scene for this period, here is an article I wrote in 2015 about the Fraser years.

The real legacy of Malcolm Fraser

Red Flag
24 March 2015

It's one of the great frauds of our time. Malcolm Fraser, wrecker of Medibank and enemy of trade unions, turned into a cuddly stuffed toy. Mourners spoke glowingly of how he had "embraced the left".

Ever the chameleon. Intellectually, Fraser was a traditional conservative, who defended standard institutions; an admirer of Keynesianism who discovered in 1976-78 that Keynesian economics had broken down by the time he was ready to grab power. This led to monetarism, which led to economic rationalism – and from there it was just a linguistic jump to the neoliberalism we know so well.

Fraser wasn't theoretically committed to any of them. He just wanted to be prime minister. In old age he returned to something like Keynesianism, because it fitted the sensibilities of the green and leftish Labor voters who gave him an audience.

For decades this fakery was about winning and holding power. More recently, no doubt, it was about the view of posterity.

Is this all too harsh? Didn't the man stand for the rights of refugees, along with land rights for Aborigines and the whole social revolution of multiculturalism?

The recent stands on refugees were real enough, but they cost the retired grazier little. The test for a politician is what he or she does in power. Fraser's approach to refugees from Vietnam in the '70s fitted neatly into anti-communist efforts to increase the right wing mood in society – right alongside his boycott of the Moscow Olympics.

I spent some of the Fraser government years scratching anti-refugee stickers off lamp posts. The Nazis who put them up could relax knowing the government wasn't campaigning against them. And the stand on refugees is the best part of Fraser.

Aborigines discovered that the seeming land rights champion used his credibility to sell them out. Facing pleas to boycott the 1982 Commonwealth Games due to the level of racism in Queensland, African states declined because they were impressed by Fraser's rhetoric on tour in Africa.

Nationally, Fraser intervened to block alliances, forcing the cancellation of a national campaign linking Aboriginal and anti-uranium activists. Aboriginal leader Galarrwuy Yunupingu described what he and his comrades faced from the Fraser government: "They threatened us. It was long, tough and hard".

Multiculturalism, closely associated with Fraser, contained another deception. It brought genuine benefits for migrants, and we have been right to defend it against right wingers.

But as Dr Robert Tierney argues, at bottom it was a strategy to contain an industrial-social rebellion that was emerging among immigrants in the factories and the inner suburbs. The strategy involved infusing each ethnic group with a monolithic identity, which in turn would take a lead from selected leaders, media and such.

It was better than traditional assimilation policies, but still designed to prop up the status quo. The relative quiescence of middle class Muslim leaders in the face of recent provocations owes something to Malcolm Fraser.

And now for the bad news. As minister for the army, he bore major responsibility for the Vietnam War. This included introducing conscription, and presiding over atrocities – at arm's length, of course. Peter Barham, a former SAS sergeant, has confirmed these happened – including water boarding.

But Fraser's biggest outrages occurred in the '70s. We will never forget the dismissal, echoing as it does other political crimes such as governor Philip Game's sacking of NSW premier Jack Lang. After Fraser took power, Liberal election ads displayed a visceral conservative arrogance toward Labor in office: "Three years of so-called working man's politicians groping around trying to handle something they were never capable of doing: running the country".

The subversion of democracy went deeper than it seemed. In normal times, the capitalist ruling class is divided on most issues. Only in crises does it mobilise in a bloc. So it was in 1975. It was Fraser's tireless campaigning that mobilised key power brokers on a class-war footing. While important for the actual sacking, governor-general John Kerr was a minor player overall.

Even more fundamental than the attacks on democracy was Fraser's onslaught on social programs. Some of this was just the usual budget cuts to be expected from conservative politicians. But when you added them up, they amounted to a reactionary social program.

And the attacks on Medibank struck at the heart of workers' hopes for a better society. Their anger was expressed in massive general strikes, contained only by the manoeuvres of trade union officials, most importantly Bob Hawke, who preferred securing social peace to winning battles.

In the aftermath, the way was open for Fraser to launch further attacks on the unions. These failed to break them, but the battles wore them out. It fell to Hawke in 1983 to strangle the traditions of Australia's mass trade union militancy. But Hawke's Accord didn't fall from the sky. It had its origins in Fraser's 1982 wage freeze.

All too typical of Malcolm Fraser in power.

Agitation, propaganda, downturn

During the 1970s, radical movements had fuelled the growth of our organisation. The unions had notched up 6 million strike days in 1977, fought the Whitlam sacking and the attacks on Medibank, and waged the long, bitter Latrobe Valley strike. Despite defeats in the Fraser era, they still came back to push strike levels up around 4 million days during the resources boom at the start of the 1980s. But there were warning signs.

The second strike wave was far less political and the union bureaucrats found it easier to control. And then the 1982-83 recession brought about a historic collapse of industrial militancy.

While the union actions had worn out the bosses to a degree, they had also worn out the industrial militants. All sides were attracted to some kind of industrial peace, and the ALP and union leaders seized the opportunity to put together a "social contract" called the ALP/ACTU Accord. The unions would stop fighting in exchange for promises of a wide range of benefits – wages, Medicare and so on. These benefits were never to arrive and workers' wages and conditions deteriorated along with unionisation rates and activism which robbed workers of their major form of defence.

The downturn continued with the deregistration of the Builders Labourers Federation in 1986, and reached its appalling conclusion when the Hawke government used the military to break a pilots' strike in 1989. The most important exception to this pattern of defeat was the 1986 Victorian nurses' strike,

JOH'S MOCK ELECTION

THE ANNOUNCEMENT that the state elections in Queensland are to be held on November 29 means that workers under Joh's thumb have the dubious privilege of playing the parliamentary game twice in one year.

The major political parties — the Liberals, Nationals and the ALP — would like us to believe that real change can come through Parliament. But in Queensland, it is doubtful that voting can even change the government.

With a gerrymander that enables Bjelke-Petersen to rule with 19% of the vote, the Labor Party is not even a serious alternative.

But despite the gerrymander, working-class action can defeat Bjelke-Petersen — *outside Parliament*.

(continued on page 3)

OUR 100th ISSUE — Feature P 6,7

the battler
PAPER OF THE INTERNATIONAL SOCIALISTS

No. 100   October 25, 1980   20 cents

Liberal snouts back in the trough

SO MALCOLM FRASER has snuffled and grunted his way back into Government for another three years.

Right away, the rest of his class — with squeals of delight — celebrated with an unprecedented buying spree on the Stock Exchange.

And right away, the Chief Pig has sunk his trotters into the middle of our backs once again.

Just two days after his election win — just 48 hours after his victory speech promising a few token training allowances for the unemployed — Fraser was back in action, launching a new attack on the 35 hour week campaign and wage indexation.

The Chief Pig wants to smash the 35 hour campaign for once and for all. He wants wage indexation hearings called off any wage indexation hearings until the ACTU drops it completely. So much for his 'concern' for creating new jobs. So much for his 'hearing the

The paper that fights for workers' power

message' of the polls.

The election campaign is over. Malcolm Fraser's Australia.

After all, if Labor had got in on Saturday, the bosses would not have accepted their authority. They would not have given up their war against us. If anything, they would have stepped it up as they did with their investment strike and their price rises under Gough Whitlam.

And Malcolm Fraser and his cohorts would have been lurking in the background, looking for any excuse to block Supply again.

The bosses don't accept our government, and there's no reason on earth why we're going to accept theirs.

Malcolm Fraser may have his snout back in the trough, but we're not going to swallow any of his swill.

years — we see no reason why workers should accept Malcolm Fraser's authority. We see no reason why we should go quiet till next election.

Matcott's View

WHY DID LABOR LOSE? — 3

Covers of The Battler *at the time*

10.7% jobless, but millions spent for —

the battler
PAPER OF THE INTERNATIONAL SOCIALISTS

No. 143 26 March, 1983   30 cents

ROYAL TWITS ON TOUR

THE HEIRS to the world's largest private fortune are currently on holiday in Australia.

Prince Charles and Diana Spencer are on holiday down in central Australia. Now that is the king holiday. But in recognition of the occasion, we are being treated to breathless reports of the Pir that sniffed air, how Willy's face, the audience on Lady Di's shorts. And all the other drivel that has to pass for news when two of the more vacuous representatives of a monstrously unequal society go on tour.

Hello suckers!

ONE MORE CUT —

the battler
PAPER OF THE INTERNATIONAL SOCIALISTS

No. 160 16 May, 1981   20 cents

FRASER'S THROAT

FRASER'S RAZOR Gang Report was only the first round of the cuts. In the next few weeks we will see round two when the State premiers start taking the knife to jobs in health and social welfare spending.

In a few short months we will have round three — the second Razor Gang Report — and that will mean more sackings, more handouts of profitable government enterprises to Fraser's wealthy friends and more savage maulings of vital public services.

MORE ON THE CUTS p 2-3

French elections

Is Mitterrand's win a victory for the left?
— see p 5

RIGHT-TO-LIFE RALLY ROUTED

IT'LL BE a long time before the Right-to-Life dares to march in Melbourne on May Day again!

A thousand pro-abortion demonstrators faced down the Right-to-Lifers outside Parliament house...

Most of the pro-abortionists had been part of the traditional May Day march and rally. A call was put out by the International Socialists, Young Gays, Gay Trade Unionists and the VPSA reform group for people to march from the Yarra Bank to Parliament House to show the...

pro-abortionists... through police... marched up Bourke... alongside the Right... marchers. A few scuffles broke out as Right-to-Lifers lost... placards, and...

At Parliament every attempt... proddlers to speak... drowned out by the... and chanting...

MAY DAY 1980
DEMONSTRATE AGAINST THE RIGHT TO LIFE

ABORTION PLATFORM

DEMONSTRATION

FREE ABORTION ON DEMAND

The Battler 17 May 1980. Report of the rally against Right to Life on May Day; leaflet advertising the rally; (opposite page) *The Battler* 26 March 1981. Article about the public service strike and rank and file group Grey Collar. Those arrested included I.S. members Pam Townshend, Di Minnis, David Main, Diane Fieldes

described in *Rebel Women*.

Industrial decline created the climate for a political drift to the right. The main protest movement at the end of the 1970s was the campaign against uranium mining, in which the spectre of union bans set the national political agenda – the bans never happened on a significant scale, but the prospect had the government seriously worried. What followed this was a bigger, but far more middle class and rather insipid movement for disarmament. It got huge crowds marching, but around very moderate politics. Other social movements fragmented, their ideas drifting towards post-modernism.

Against this background the IS began to run into difficulties. In the 1970s the group had operated on a perspective of continuing crisis and mass struggle, expecting a bigger revolutionary movement to grow out of rank and file work in industry and militant campaigns. We saw ourselves primarily as agitators. We didn't confine ourselves to this: on the contrary we published a theoretical journal and sometimes had quite theoretical debates. But like the rest of our international tendency, and with the encouragement of the British SWP, we emphasised agitation.

The perspectives adopted at the founding conference of the IS in 1975 were based on the assumption of rapidly deepening social crisis and considerable prospects for building

150 I.S. in Australia: the 1980s

the IS into a larger organisation. In the event, we overestimated both. As a consequence, we soon found that our attempts to maintain a fortnightly paper were floundering since we lacked a large enough membership base to sustain it. Our "industrialisation" program soon collapsed. The group subsequently arrived at the view that industrialisation – sending students into factories – is not the best way to build working class influence anyway. After various changes in the frequency of the paper it eventually settled down to a three-weekly schedule.

We thought we had grown because of our interventions in the working class, but in reality we had recruited very few industrial militants, and those who had joined us were generally tertiary-educated public servants or teachers. Moreover, we had recruited them to complex Marxist ideas, which related to the role of the working class in socialist revolution – ideas which appeared more credible to them because of the high levels of class struggle, and our resulting ability to mix with militant workers.

The downturn in class struggle after 1982 forced a rethink of our overall strategy.

Aware of the traditional Marxist distinctions between agitation (arguing relatively simple ideas to a mass audience) and propaganda (arguing complex ideas to a small audience), we were suspicious of doing too much of the latter. This was because we thought propaganda was abstract. We didn't understand how the high levels of class struggle had enabled us to make *concrete propaganda* arguments in a popular style, pointing to immediate events in the struggle, but carrying wider lessons. At our best we did this, but we didn't draw general lessons.

SEVENTY picketers outside the Government Centre in Sydney voting for a motion calling on the officials to organise further strike action and meetings against the CERR Act. Shortly after, four of their number were arrested. Since then two more activists, Di Minnis (top) and Pam Townshend, have been since summonsed.

In the 1980s these underlying contradictions were exposed. By early 1981 we wrote of a shift to the right and by the following year we had begun to grasp how serious it was. I wrote in an internal document:

> The external climate has offered few opportunities for significant recruitment...Whereas we could say a year ago that the majority of the left was moving rightwards, but a minority

> was being polarised our way, we must now accept that [this minority] is tending to dry up.

Suggestions that we see ourselves more as a "propaganda group" came initially from a minority of the leadership and membership, including me. We were influenced by a new British perspective which spoke of a "downturn", soon to be written with a capital "D", but more importantly by a dislike of a culture of artificial stunts and street fighting, especially in Melbourne. This culture had emerged as the real struggle began to fade.

The IS had an orientation of confronting right-wing anti-abortion groups, and this began quite well when Right to Life (a "pro-life" group) foolishly held a rally in Melbourne on May Day in 1980. The traditional May Day rally brought crowds of leftists into the streets, and the IS was the main group mobilising a thousand of these to counter demonstrate.

Charging past police horses, we headed up Bourke Street to Parliament House, where we pushed our way into the anti-abortion crowd. While the anti-abortionists were more numerous, many of them such as the families bussed in after Sunday mass were hardly prepared for a street battle. Finding themselves eyeball to eyeball with chanting leftists, they dispersed. Because we had mobilised large numbers, the action did not need to get violent at all. The stand-out event was watching Rose Stone (Janey's mother) pull down the enemy's loudspeaker.

Later actions were far smaller, yet a cult of street-fighting began to emerge, where some leaders argued there were times when only "military" considerations mattered. This was dangerous. Confrontation is only useful if we keep it political. Tiny groups were substituting our own energy and organisation for mass action.

In the early 1980s the IS leadership had confronted localised oppositions in some branches, mainly in Melbourne and Brisbane, and fought them hard by mobilising their own supporters. In the process we lost some important activists with significant roots in the outside world. These losses were a sign that we were becoming more isolated from the world around us; at the same time it isolated us further.

The conflicts were a warning. They also helped set the scene for the later organisation-wide faction fight in 1984, by demonstrating the power of internal mobilisation against critics. After the Brisbane split, I wrote that various local conflicts had "precipitated out something of a real national cadre" in what had previously been a very federal organisation. While acknowledging the positives, I warned that "given the context of the internal struggles of the past period, it may be perceived as a kind of 'leadership faction'. Worse,…elements of it may actually tend to see themselves that way." Not only did that happen, but sections of the cadre began to see all critics as right wingers full of "rotten ideas".

The leadership then proposed radical changes in our work. In People for Nuclear Disarmament for example. we were no longer to play a constructive role, rather we should have a much more cavalier attitude to the meetings and see them mainly as an opportunity to train new members. Some of us were concerned about this downgrading of social movements and campaigns. We also felt the organisation was increasingly inward-looking and subjecting members to an authoritarian regime.

I identified this as the politics of impatience – how the group, confronted by a situation of downturn in class struggle in the 1980s, was impatient for something to happen, and tried to make up for this lack by artificially creating activity within the group.

Here is Rick Kuhn's summary of my approach:

> Flair, risk-taking and innovation in relating to new developments have a place, he acknowledges. Sustained attempts to force the pace of events in unfavourable circumstances, which Tom identified as the politics of impatience, do not.

> As the levels of social struggle declined, a majority of the leadership of the IS had become impatient with the group's membership and the world outside. The result was voluntarism; attempts to substitute the organisation's determination for the inadequacies of the real world: intolerance of internal disagreement and anything less than the very high level of activity expected of members, a sectarian attitude to serious movements and others involved in them; and a predilection for self-generated campaigns that drew in very few other people.[16]

We set up a formal faction and the dispute reached a climax at the conference in 1984, where we lost the vote about 60-40. After a further period of conflict, most of us oppositionists left the IS in mid-August 1985 to form a new organisation, Socialist Action.

A young Hegelian?

Meanwhile, throughout the 1980s, I had tried to deepen my understanding of Marxism by a program of reading and discussion. In late 1982 I was in the UK for the SWP Conference. I met with many leaders and members of the SWP, including Ian Birchall, Duncan Hallas, Nigel Harris, Chris Harman, Peter Binns, Pete Goodwin, Colin Sparks and Alex Callinicos. In a letter to Janey I noted:

> All the leadership are friendly enough, but very busy. I have to keep pushing myself forward, at the risk of being regarded as a pain in the arse, otherwise I will keep getting forgotten... The rank and file are very friendly however, and seem remarkably interested in Australia and the IS – partly because the miners smashing up the doors of parliament in Canberra was big news here.

I met and spent time with Tony Cliff and his partner Chanie Rosenberg:

> She is a powerful personality in her own right, though when Cliff is in the room even she is eclipsed... I went to their place for dinner and listened to Cliff (it was nominally a conversation) for several hours. He is an absolute bundle of energy. The most interesting thing was that I heard all these stories, all these ideas, etc. – and the next day they were all in his speech at conference. He lives his politics all day long. At conference he towered over everyone, and no one objected to his regular interventions.

At the end of that year and January the following year I was in Walnut Creek for some weeks. My brother was diagnosed with bowel cancer and died very quickly. Living for weeks with my parents, I had a lot of spare time and used it to read. From letters to Janey:

> I have been studying hard. After reading sections of Hegel, plus massive amounts of commentary, I got hold of CLR James' "Notes on Dialectic" and studied it for days. It is very hard to master. For a break, I [read] "An Introduction to Philosophy" which goes through some basic Aristotle etc. I read everything through, take notes, then go out for a walk to clear my head.
>
> I've just been bombarding my poor head with so much stuff it doesn't all go in smoothly at first. I got hold of the German originals of [Hegel's] *Logic*…amazingly enough I can read it, though it is a slog. The German is easier than the English because the translations are so ambiguous and stilted. This will be great – with Hegel I can outwank ANYBODY.

Developing my newly acquired ideas, I wrote a piece I called "the strangest thing I've ever written", which probably remains true. It was an attempt to apply what I had learned about the dialectic from reading in Hegel to what was then called "the multi-issue approach" and today would be called intersectionality. I wrote about what I called the "methodology of the shopping list" as compared to the Hegelian dialectic.

I discussed how Hegel starts with what he calls analytical cognition, a basic level of thinking, in which, for example, we notice that there are men and women, blacks and whites, workers and bosses in the world. We then move up to recognising the connections between these attributes: "men oppress women, whites oppress blacks, and black women are oppressed twice. Black women workers are oppressed three times while rich women are only oppressed once. This is synthetic cognition, which reaches its culmination with the blinding insight that all these things are 'inter-related'."

> This synthetic cognition is an entirely necessary step, but it is limited. The connections are real and to establish them is necessary but they are external connections, mechanical connections… There is nothing which makes these things move, no dynamic. There is no way for one thing to give rise to another, transcend another, let alone smash another. It is just a shopping list, even with all the "inter-relationships".

Tom, Easter 1984

Hegel accepts that synthetic cognition is a necessary step, but he is scathing about people who get stuck there. For serious minds the shopping list soon loses its appeal. As Hegel says, "The trick of such wisdom is learned as quickly as it is easy to master it; its repetition, once it is known, becomes as insufferable as the repetition of a sleight of hand one sees through".

I quoted Hegel's attack on this way of thinking.

> It would be difficult to decide what is greater – the smugness with which everything in the heavens, on earth, and beneath the earth is coated with such a broth of paint, or the conceit that is based on the supposed excellence of this panacea: each supports the other. The product of this method of labelling everything in heaven and earth, all natural and spiritual forms, with a few determinations of the general schema, and thus pigeonholing everything, (amounts to) a tabulation that is like a skeleton with little pieces of paper stuck all over it, or like the rows of closed, labelled jars in a spicer's stall… flesh and blood are removed from the bones…the living essence of the matter is left out.[17]

I continued to lambast people on the left who fall into this trap for some paragraphs and then acknowledged that it was time "I at least hinted at the alternative to all this mechanical thinking". That alternative is that synthetic cognition must be overcome by a dialectic in which, for example, working women can leap into the leadership of class struggles. I then admitted that I had only read as far as the Preface to *The Phenomenology of Mind*, so my understanding was still raw: "Probably I have butchered Hegel." I did however note that the "dialectic explains how and why things move, and how people transform themselves."

156 I.S. in Australia: the 1980s

MINES AND MASS RALLIES: LATIN AMERICA 1985

Peru and Bolivia

Janey and I went on a trip to South America in mid-1985, visiting Ecuador, Peru and Bolivia with two friends, Helen Rosenberg and Deborah Rosenberg, and afterwards moving on to Nicaragua.

I wrote in the diary I kept of the trip:

> All the way down from San Francisco and Miami I nursed a secret fear. After playing the role of Spanish teacher with, no doubt, a bit of posturing, would I be able to perform with the language? It hasn't been too bad so far. At the airport I had to get rid of importunate taxi-drivers, and by gosh they went away when I told them to... The real problem has not been speaking (I can rattle off a few pat phrases all too well) but understanding the reply. Sometimes I do and feel a rush of confidence. Sometimes it all rattles past me.

In Ecuador we had a pleasant visit to the little town of Baños, travelling by bus.

> The bus was a little bit like a sardine can, and the seats certainly weren't designed with someone my size in mind, and two people got sick and had to get out and throw up. But otherwise it was a pleasant trip through some fairly spectacular mountain scenery. A little sign at the front of the bus announced very politely: "Dear Mr Passenger, please throw your litter out the window", but...I kept my litter until we got here and found a trash can.

Military rule in Peru had ended in 1979, and we were there during a presidential election, won by the leftist Alan García. There was a lot of social unrest. The other political context was the activity of the guerrilla group *Sendero Luminoso* (Shining Path). They were mainly active in the countryside, but also had an impact in urban areas.

> Shortly after our arrival [in Lima] Janey and Helen saw a demonstration of strikers, and then in a church we came across a dozen or so hunger strikers from the fishermen's union. Originally 19 went on hunger strike but some have been taken to hospital. The strikers are demanding a better system of payment as well as the re-opening of a state factory. The other day we read there had been a fairly violent and successful general strike in Chimbote in their support.
>
> All but me went to the pictures. About 9 pm the film stopped for a few minutes. Back at our pension the lights flickered as I sat reading. It later emerged that Sendero Luminoso had knocked out the power in much of the city, then used the darkness to launch bomb attacks at (among others) the US, Russian and Chinese embassies…
>
> It was in Lima also that I finally found a left-wing paper, the Communist Party's *Unidad*. I found it near a university or college of some sort, which is perhaps not an accident. It seems many of the campuses are left wing centres – indeed the government is using the pretext that Sendero Luminoso is active there to crack down on the whole left on campus. Dozens of radical students have been rounded up for "questioning".

After a flying visit to the Amazon in the interior of Peru, a highlight of our trip, we finally managed to make contact with a left wing group in Cusco.

> As the left faces ongoing repression, it does not advertise the location of its various offices. We began with the address of a church-run study centre. This was not, of course, at the address we had been given but we were directed onward and eventually found it. After some initial explanation a person was found who knew the whereabouts of <u>one</u> leftist party… It was located in a street called San Andrea, in the third block.
>
> Along we went to that block and searched every sign and doorway. Nothing. We entered a squalid courtyard and climbed rickety steps

Tom, Janey, Helen and Deborah in the Amazon jungle near Iquitos, Peru, 1985; Tom with Jane Tovey in Bolivia July 2009

to a trade union office, however, and they had heard of the PUM. "It's in the second block, halfway up." A thorough search of the second block revealed precisely nothing so we entered the premises of a human rights organisation, who finally gave us an exact address. In through an archway we went, up some stairs and there it was: the offices of the PUM.

Carlos was an economist who also worked with the campesino (peasant) movement. He gave us several hours out of his busy schedule and was a thoroughly likeable fellow.

The PUM (*Partido Unificado Mariateguista*, Mariateguist Unified Party) was Peru's largest Marxist (used loosely) party. It had been founded in 1984 by a fusion of a number of leftists and revolutionary organisations. At the elections that took place shortly before we arrived in 1985 the PUM were part of the United Left ticket.

From Peru we went to Bolivia. According to the postcard I sent my parents, it took "a 9 hour bus journey with some fairly comical scenes at the border and on the bus". The currency was inflating at an incredible pace – 330,000 Bolivian pesos to the US dollar.

Our next political encounter was in La Paz, capital of Bolivia, where we were very keen to meet up with some political activists in this country, which has an inspiring history of struggle.

I proceed to the Miners' Federation Office. We had been there the other day, and met some friendly miners from a pit threatened with closure. Then we got to see an official, who promised us a letter of recommendation to the Oruro office. We were to return at 2.30 on Tuesday to get it, and we gave up a tour to do so. On my arrival I ask for Compañero Cortes. Cortes knows nothing about a letter and will not give me one. "But there is no problem. You can go everywhere and talk to everyone. Journalists do it all the time."

Disgruntled I walk on to the offices of *Aquí*, a leftist weekly whose staff are extremely friendly. Satisfaction at last.

A couple of days later, Janey and I took the bus to Oruro, a major mining town, well off the beaten tourist track.

Oruro is a rather sad little city. We tramped the streets looking for hotels, only to find that none had showers or hot water. Finally we got a room in the "Ideal", which was far from that, but it had hot water of sorts in a communal shower. Restaurants worthy of the name amount to one, the "Pigalle" on the main square… The town was also very cold and as we rose early we suffered.

But we had come to meet miners and if possible go down a mine so we set our sights on that.

On the day we arrived we headed for the Miners' Federation HQ, which is inside the gates of the state mining firm COMIBOL. The local secretary said there would be a press conference next day at 10 am and a regional delegates' meeting, as well as food distribution to the worker's families.

At 9.30 next day we rolled up to see queues of people getting bread and other staples from a window. A union delegate offered to show us around and we found the shelves were terribly bare. There are shortages of everything. Before we could proceed further the manager of the "supermarket" arrived, a self-important man who chewed out the delegate for not consulting him. A row ensued, and the unionist departed. But at any rate we had seen enough.

We went up to the union office. The press conference, set for 10, showed no sign of happening, but we got to talk to the union secretary from Siglo XX, famed centre of working class struggle. And finally, as we were being informed the press conference was cancelled, we met the only other journalist present – a pleasant man from the Revolutionary Workers' Party (POR). After a talk with him over coffee, we arranged to meet again that evening and headed for the bus terminal, where we caught a local bus up to the little mining town of Huanuni.

This was a real mining town, dominated by the mine and generally rather grim. To reach it we travelled through clouds of dust over a bumpy dirt road. Once there, we marched boldly through the COMIBOL gates and found the union office.

Once again we got a very friendly reception. On the wall, two pictures of (Indigenous) rebels. They told us of their hardship – wages of $20 a month. And they couldn't even get decent coca leaves to chew. As we talked a big bag of leaves was brought in – black, hard to chew, they said. Nowadays all the good coca goes to the cocaine trade.

That evening, back in Oruro, our man from the POR took us to the local campus. It was a scene of frantic activity, as rival groups chanted and sang in support of their tickets in the student elections. Huge portraits of Marx, Lenin, Trotsky and Che Guevara adorned the walls. On learning we were "Trotskyists" of a sort the young POR people asked me what was the state of negotiations between Guyillermo Lora and the Fourth International. I said we were not from the 4th International, but rather from the IS. "Ah, Tony Cliff."

Due to the ubiquity of ballot box stuffing, there was a rule that an election was still legal as long as no more than one third of votes were invalid.

The *Partido Obrero Revolucionario* (POR, Revolutionary Workers Party) had been the first Trotskyist party in Bolivia. In a serendipitous coincidence, it was originally called the Marxist Workers Group, but had changed its name in 1946.

We had heard we could visit the San Jose mine just outside Oruro.

> At the Tourist Information Office we were told to rise early and get micro-bus D. Rise early we did, on our last day – about 6.30 am. My god it was cold. We stood about for half an hour on the appropriate street corner but microbus D did not appear. Finally we got a taxi to the mine and

asked for the manager. He was not there so we wandered about, until finally his underling called us and said, apologetically, that we could not go down the mine that day. The day before, it seemed, a government commission had done so and the workers were a little annoyed.

So at 7.45 we walked downhill from the mine in the shadow of the great slag heap, past the dismal dwellings of the miners, and caught a bus back to town.

I noted in my diary that "in Oruro there was a chicken shortage". Chicken was our staple meal, and it was quite disconcerting, upon ordering "*pollo*" to hear "*no hay*" – there isn't any. "But then in Oruro everything was short."

One outcome of this South American trip was our discovery of the Peruvian Marxist, Jose Carlos Mariátegui, a socialist and Communist in the 1920s, who wrote one of the first materialist analyses of a Latin American society. Mariátegui, who died in 1930, had an enormous influence on the whole left in Peru. In the election that we witnessed, nearly everyone appealed to his traditions.

You can read the article I subsequently wrote about Mariátegui online at Tom O'Lincoln's Red Sites.

Revolutionary
mural in Managua

Nicaragua

In May-July 1979, the people of Nicaragua overthrew one of Latin America's most hated dictators, President Anastasio Somoza. It was the culmination of a guerrilla insurgency combined with urban insurrection. It cost tens of thousands of lives to win democracy.

The revolutionaries identified with the tradition of Augusto Sandino, leader of an insurgency in the 1920s and early 1930s that fought the US Marines occupying Nicaragua. The new regime maintained a mixed economy. It wasn't communism, yet that didn't save them from a murderous CIA-funded invasion in the 1980s.

As late as 1984, Sandinista National Liberation Front (FSLN) leader Daniel Ortega won a presidential poll with 67 percent of the vote. With the Sandinistas still defying the might of US imperialism, Janey and I went to see the revolution for ourselves.

We were there for 17 days in June and July 1985. We stayed in a small hotel, but ate many meals at the Hotel Intercontinental, a major landmark. The buffet was famous – it was known as the "Interswine" because everyone pigged out at this all-you-can-eat event. My diary recorded our experiences.

> After a few days in Nicaragua my main reaction is that the revolution is way in the past. What exists now is a war. The government shows some signs of fatigue, strain, erratic behaviour. Take the currency. The official rate is 28 to the dollar. At this rate, breakfast at the Intercontinental Hotel costs $US14.10. The black market rate has soared far beyond this. In May, the government

163 Mines and mass rallies: Latin America 1985

decided to legalise the black market since it cannot control it. On Thursday the government-run green shack outside the Intercontinental was buying dollars at 650:1. But today, Saturday, the rate had fallen to 400 at the green shack.

"I have very precise instructions" said the man. "You can get 650 on the back market in the Carreterría a Masaya but not here."

I described our *pension* in the diary.

The barrio west of the Intercontinental Hotel is known to the locals as "Gringolandia" and with good reason. It is the main centre for "hospedajes" [hostels] and the particular sort of "comedor" [café]… which caters mostly to gringos.

The pension Dorado, adjacent to the Cine Dorado and the El Dorado ice cream parlour, is a ramshackle building with thin partitions between rooms (you can hear *everything*). We were lucky – we got a room with a window, though to get it we had to go upstairs. This not only meant it was hotter, it also meant we got an especially strong dose of the juke box which played til all hours in the beer joint around the corner.

The roosters began to crow non-stop each morning. And the intervening hours of the night were accounted for by barking dogs. Two days a week there was no water (the influx of refugees from the northern war zone has overstrained the water supply and the government has resorted to rationing)…big buckets of water were provided.

We weren't long in Nicaragua, but we spent all of the time tramping around Managua or travelling, including to Grenada and to León. Our first day we spent marching around in the hot sun. Managua was an incredibly decentralised city and it was impossible to find anything. We tried to get press credentials, only to find they were too expensive.

Going to the International Press Club we managed to join an excursion to the northern front line area of the contra war.

After a 6.30 am breakfast we piled into the minibus and drove north for two hours. This took us to Matagalpa where we got a press conference with Sandinista reps explaining the resettlement of people relocated away from the border… Somoza used to recruit guardsmen up here – a lot of them are now with the contras.

> Many families are quite divided. The government people did not hide these facts.

From Matagalpa we proceeded up into the mountains to visit (temporary) refugee camps and more permanent settlements, where we saw few people as most were out working.

> Huge pigs rooted around. Houses were made out of raw concrete, but looked no worse than some housing we've seen in Managua.

My diary recounts the state of our stomachs, as we had had very little to eat during the day.

> Finally about 7 pm we got into Matagalpa and a debate ensued over whether we should stop for food. Sanity prevailed, and chicken sandwiches and milk shakes saved our lives.

> At Jinotega we saw a line of maybe 20 trucks waiting to go in convoy to the area we had left. Why go at night? Who knows.

On the bus, we talked to a Reuters photographer, Louis, who had been in Nicaragua five months. On this Press Club excursion, most of the participants were like us – "alternative". Louis was the sole rep from mainstream media. He was sympathetic to the FSLN but honest, intelligent and critical. He told us how the government "messes the journos around dreadfully".

> One day they were told they'd be shown some villages attacked by contras. They were put into buses, driven for two hours, then shown a map. No villages. The real purpose was to take them and their cameras through some other town to prove it was not occupied by the enemy.

The International Press Club was very handy for us in a number of ways: we got to hear a presentation by Enrique Bolaños (then head of the bosses' organisation COSEP[18]) and also by Carlos Nuñez, one of the nine members of the ruling directorate. Nuñez showed up 30 minutes late:

> He was an amiable, boyish-looking fellow, young for his job as are most of the Commandantes. He mixed easily with journos, very unpretentious. Outside in the street a body guard with a machine gun.

Elsewhere we met with FSLN cadres and political dissidents ranging

from Trotskyists and Maoists through to the main legal conservative party. Gerardo Alfaro, one of the conservative party leaders, was adamant that the US would not invade because "it must surely have learned the lessons of Vietnam". Asked what they would do if the US did invade he said, "We will all fight."

One fellow I met in the street brightly informed me that the US was going to "start bombing us on 4 July". I dismissed him as a crank until I saw the same story on the front page of a newspaper. My diary again:

> In the streets around Managua, the most recent war scare has caused the deployment of tanks. In some places they are digging fox-holes. How much good this sort of conventional defence will be if the US invades one wonders. But perhaps the government is doing it to make the public feel an effort is being made.

166   **Mines and mass rallies: Latin America 1985**

Children in a town visited during excursion to Matagalpa; (opposite page) building displaying "Sandino lives" poster; selling drinks through the windows of the bus

We hoped we had made a tiny contribution to forestalling an invasion by joining a picket in front of the US embassy. The US had invaded Grenada two years previously, on the pretext that they were there to protect American civilians. As a result of that, all the Americans in Nicaragua turned up once a month to a demonstration, with placards saying things like "We do not need to be rescued!"

I read all the newspapers and commented in my diary:

> *Barricada* is easily the best-written and designed official government paper in the world, probably because it has to compete with *La Prensa*. Even so [it] is very one-dimensional and one is glad *La Prensa* is available.
>
> *La Prensa* is more sensational and has the sort of "non-political" news that the average citizen likes. It also pushes some right wing politics but very gingerly. One wonders how much is being censored. *El Nuevo Diario* is a *Barricada* clone.
>
> On arriving at Sandino airport on my way out, I bought a copy of *El Nuevo Diario*. The paper condemned Honduras for spreading lies about Nicaraguan attacks on that country.

167 **Mines and mass rallies: Latin America 1985**

Bonifacio Miranda, member of PRT (Workers Revolutionary Party) selling El Socialista outside Fanatex – Nicaragua's largest textile factory; (opposite page) monthly demonstrations of Americans

Two hours later, my plane lands in Honduras, a man gets on with a paper, and what's the headline? "Rain of Nicaraguan bombs on Honduran territory".

We set out to meet up with the PRT, a party aligned with the Fourth International. This was not easy.

Finding anything in Managua is impossible. There are no street names or numbers. To find the Partido Revolucionario de los Trabajadores [Workers Revolutionary Party] we had to follow these directions which appeared in their newspaper (which we came across it at a bookstall in the Huembes Market). "From the Marxist-Leninist bookshop go half a block toward the lake." The taxi driver had a hard time finding the bookshop, but from there it was a piece of cake.

Bonifacio Miranda, who spoke to us, looked every inch the intellectual Trotskyist. Later when we saw him selling the paper (El Socialista) outside the Fanatex factory, we were impressed with his enthusiasm.

It was better talking to oppositionists of any sort than to most Sandinistas (the party line gets tedious even if you agree with it). One exception was Sandra at AMNLAE [Luisa Amanda Espinoza Association of Nicaraguan Women] who has a hint of feminism about her despite her formally party-line views.

We attended a mass rally commemorating the retreat to Masaya – an event during the 1979 insurrection that laid the basis for victory. There were perhaps 50,000 people present and the mood was jolly more than militant.

168   Mines and mass rallies: Latin America 1985

Ortega appeared as keynote speaker. The slouching, intellectual-looking president with his glasses and droopy moustache was curiously appealing next to the ramrod-stiff military dignitaries who accompanied him. He was introduced with full flourishes:

El Presidente de la Republica!
Miembro de la Dirección Nacional del FSLN!
Commandante de la Revolución!
Daniel Ortega Saavedra!

From Tom's diary:

> To appreciate the full flavour of this, you have to imagine a booming and somewhat theatrical voice, with every "r" being trilled until you think the man's tongue is going to fall off. Daniel's speaking style is mediocre. Half the crowd listened. The working class was not mentioned once.

During his speech the crowd chanted: "*Aquí, allá, el Yanqui morirá!*" (Whether here or there, the Yankees will die!) That sounded serious enough. The Sandinista anthem blared out: "*Luchamos contra el Yanqui – Enemigo de la humanidad!*" (We fight against the Yankee – enemy of humanity.) Ortega emphasised that the attack on enemies of humanity was directed against the US imperialists, not ordinary people. Then he asked: "Are there North Americans here?" A scattering of hands went up; I put mine up, I guess I'm an American. Ortega declared: "These are brothers and sisters of the

Mass rally to commemorate 1979 retreat to Masaya; (opposite page) Daniel Ortega addresses the rally

Nicaraguan people" (cheers).

In 1985 there was still hope the government might survive. Much rested on the economy, and workers' relationship to it. In Nicaragua's mixed economy, big business was still entrenched, and the FSLN promoted it. As the Central American Historical Institute noted in a 1981 paper, "[T]he state financial system…helped with 100 percent of the requirements of the private sector in terms of working capital and investment – considerably more than Somoza".

The state sector was also important, because it influenced the pace of national development. Yet an enterprise does not become socialist simply because it is run by the state. Agriculture minister Jaime Wheelock told managers:

> The state enterprises have to be models of economic rationality. They have to be profitable. They are not… enterprises to make social services for the community. They have costs and they have to make a profit, and the costs are rising and so the prices have to go up.[19]

So the new forms of production looked much like the old ones. State enterprises were subordinated to the demands of profitability: pricing was dictated by market forces, not human needs, and tomorrow's investment depended on today's rate of return.

Some big landholdings were rightly taken over by the state or parcelled out to the peasants, in a radical land reform. Nevertheless, the growth of a peasantry, even if organised into cooperatives, is an essentially capitalist affair. As explained by the daily *El Nuevo Diario*, it creates "not a collectivist but a middle class consciousness".

The absence of nationalised industry did not have to prevent the Sandinista regime from heading for socialism. The Bolshevik plan after the Russian Revolution was not to carry out extensive nationalisations (though these were imposed on

170 Mines and mass rallies: Latin America 1985

them by events), and they knew that alone they could not construct socialism. They needed help from revolutions elsewhere.

The Bolshevik orientation was above all political. The decisive step towards socialism in an underdeveloped nation was for the workers to take power – consistent with Marx's declaration, "The first step in the revolution by the working class is to raise the proletariat to the position of ruling class, to win the battle for democracy." But this wasn't on the agenda in Nicaragua.

The government was in line with Western-style parliamentarism. Unlike the 1917 Soviet regime, there were no workers' councils through which the proletariat exercised power. This parliamentary system represented a huge step forward for people previously oppressed by a dictator. But it had no specifically socialist character.

Most sympathetic observers conceded as much, but pointed to other features that allegedly added a dimension of mass democracy. One writer spoke of the "seeds of genuine democracy" being sown in the factories, farms and schools. Mass organisations, such as the Sandinista Defence Committees (CDS) and the women's organisation AMNLAE, were an important arm of FSLN political power. So were the unions. But a closer examination shows the power relations were controlled from above.

The leadership wanted to know what people thought, to which end Daniel Ortega held a "Face the People" session about once a week, a real opportunity for people to express their views. However, the decision as to whether to act on these views rested with the government. Critical comments were increasing, provoking grumbling from the FSLN and proposals to orchestrate the whole affair.

Representatives of both CDS and AMNLAE told me their main role was to support the decisions of the FSLN leadership. They spoke of how people mobilised to boost production and solve problems, but neither women nor youth had real leverage in the political process. The AMNLAE representative expressed considerable frustration with her organisation's inability to make headway.

The CDS neighbourhood committees were extensive, comprising some 50,000 block committees. They distributed necessities at controlled prices and engaged in "revolutionary vigilance". But they didn't make the key decisions. This is quite clear from Tomás Borge's speech to CDS activists:

> What has the National Directorate determined to be the principal task of the Sandinista Defence Committees? You have said it: revolutionary vigilance! Why did the National Directorate determine that the principal and fundamental task of the Sandinista Defence Committees would be revolutionary vigilance? To a great extent…because reality has shown that the main responsibility of Nicaraguans at this ominous hour is the defence of our nation.[20]

Assuming this was a good decision, it is still clear it was made not by the committees themselves but by the National Directorate, in whose selection the CDS had no voice. Hence the slogan, "National Directorate, give the order!", which was commonly shouted at rallies.

There was much talk of "workers' participation" and sometimes workers' control. This gave the impression that employees had a say. Not so. At one time there was real workers' control, because during and shortly after the revolution, when employers left the country or began to decapitalise their firms, workers were compelled to seize factories to keep them running, and often did so with the blessing of the FSLN. By the time we arrived, however, all managers were firmly in control.

Workers continued to "participate", but their participation was limited. The aim was to draw the workforce into the drive for production. The "enterprise committees" consisted of representatives of management, the workers and the FSLN reps. In such a "troika" the workers had a minority voice.

Perhaps the closest thing to grassroots democracy on the job was the periodic workplace assemblies. Yet the FSLN union paper *Trabajadores* indicated that here, too, democracy didn't go very deep:

> In recent days there took place a production assembly at CECALSA, where the director of the enterprise, Denis Lopez, made known the production plans of the firm for this year as well as individual and collective production goals. For its part, the union made known the commitments of the workers to ending labour indiscipline, augmenting production, strengthening defence and taking forward the innovators' movement with the standardisation of work.[21]

The boss did not ask but told the workers what was to be done; the union pledged to keep the workers' noses to the grindstone.

Times were hard due to the US blockade. There was a fair bit of grumbling about inflation and shortages. From my diary:

> There were shortages of basic goods. In the supermarket people were limited to two rolls of toilet paper each.

> One day I was sitting in a stationary taxi when a man walked by with tins of powdered milk. "Hey, where'd you get the milk?" the driver called. Moments later someone walked past with soap. "Hey," yelled the taxi driver, "where'd you get the soap?"

Attacked on all sides, the revolution called on workers and peasants to sacrifice. But austerity's legitimacy depends on the regime. It's one thing for a government representing the working class to demand sacrifices from workers. It's another if demands are made by a regime beyond their control, which uses some of the proceeds to boost profits.

Real wages had already fallen dramatically, due to the effects of natural disasters and war. In August 1984 the government partially removed subsidies on prices of basic necessities, and in February 1985 they were abolished. The consequence was a wave of inflation.

The shops selling basic necessities

in factories had been abolished, to be replaced with centralised "supermarkets", but it seemed clear workers would suffer. In addition, the government abolished the so-called "payment in kind" through which workers could buy some products made in their enterprise at cost price. The FSLN argued with considerable logic that this practice worsened inflation. They said it was politically corrupting, being essentially speculation. Nevertheless, ending "payment in kind" brought cuts in workers' incomes and provoked strikes.

When workers challenged him, Ortega attacked "ultra-left parties" that were "strengthening the forces of imperialism". At the E. Chamorro factory in Granada, workers occupied the plant in June 1985, only to be kicked out by police.

Agricultural labourers were also under pressure. The problem was that after the revolution, the labourers and their unions successfully demanded reductions in workload. Wheelock responded in 1985 by demanding the workers double their output:

> The [sugar workers] can't sow 600 shoots of cane as they are doing today, they have to sow the 1,200 they sowed previously, and if possible they have to sow 1,400 for the revolution. Because the Somoza regime got 1,200 out of the workers.[22]

Nobody makes a revolution in order to increase workloads. In 1991, confronted with pressures like these, Nicaraguans voted for the political alternative. It was a defeat. The wearing effect of years of war and isolation had taken their toll. Sandinista activists let tears flow as they surveyed the wreckage. But it was a defeat within a liberal democratic system. And bringing liberal democracy to Nicaragua was an undoubted victory.

An incident I have never forgotten. Drinking beer after work is a simple exercise – I'm a pretty basic drinker and surroundings don't have to be fancy. In Nicaragua, I quickly I found a basic beer joint well filled with beer-joint denizens. I settled down to drink and read the paper. A boy skulked into the room, cadging money. I brushed him aside. He returned, persistent. I brushed him aside. This time one of the denizens responded. Unsteady on his feet, he stood proudly erect and told me off. "Señor, we in Nicaragua have made a revolution. We did not make it so you, Señor, can brush our children aside." In a moment the episode was over, leaving two emotions. So ashamed of myself. So proud of them.

Writing about Nicaragua

Much of the above analysis is taken from a pamphlet I wrote upon our return, which attempted to provide a theoretical backing to my impressions from the visit.

Nearly two decades later, in July 2004, I commented about Nicaragua on the Marxmail internet discussion list, prompting moderator Louis Proyect to refer me to his own assessment and suggest that if I had other views, I might write my own.

Because my line of argument was not fashionable and would meet considerable resistance, I based a lot of the text on published material (as much as possible on Sandinista sources) that could be referenced and therefore be harder to dismiss. But the pamphlet was also based on some first-hand observation and discussions I had in the country. I felt this was an important component of my contribution.

Lou did not think that my personal experiences were all that relevant. He suggested my analysis should be "scholarly"; and that it wasn't really important to have visited Nicaragua in person. In some ways I sympathise with this sentiment. The world is too full of lefties who fly in and out of places and claim a spurious authority. But on the other hand, going and having a look really does enhance your understanding, at least if you have the language skills to talk widely to people. I do agree that we need rigour in our arguments and did my best in that regard, but then again perhaps too many "scholarly" pretensions bring their own dangers.

In commenting on someone else's work Lou also wrote: "There are

Tom and Janey relaxing in the lobby of the Intercontinental Hotel

strong grounds for seeing [the revolution's] defeat not so much in terms of its lacking revolutionary fibre, but being outgunned by far superior forces." I have a lot of sympathy with this view too. Morally, the blame lies with US imperialism. Practically speaking, huge imperialist pressures were the most important factor in the Sandinistas' demise. But this does not mean there is no value in considering other factors, as I tried to do in my pamphlet.

I don't mean it was my job to tell the Nicaraguans what they "should have" done. That would be silly. I had no great achievements to make me an authority, and no reason to think any Nicaraguans were going to read what I wrote. It was really about exploring the meaning of socialism itself for a small audience in Australia. Nevertheless it may have some value in understanding what happened in Nicaragua.

I republished some sections of the pamphlet on my own website Red Sites, with much of the above as introduction. At the end of the extracts I made the point that the problems did not diminish in the slightest our responsibility to display principled solidarity with the Sandinistas against imperialist aggression.

I also quoted a remark by Nicaraguan president Daniel Ortega that gives an insight into where the FSLN thought it was heading:

> Perhaps the Nicaraguan revolution is something that can be compared to the Algerian revolution. In the context of Latin America, we would see it as being close to what the Mexican process has been.[23]

My response (slightly edited) was:

> Ortega (must have known) that both revolutions had ended up with the institutionalisation of the revolutionaries as top-down ruling parties; in the Mexican case they even called themselves the "Institutionalised Revolutionary Party" Neither revolution took on a socialist direction.

176   Mines and mass rallies: Latin America 1985

I.S. IN AUSTRALIA: SOCIALIST ACTION 1985-89

Following the faction fight in 1984 over the "politics of impatience", about a third of the membership left to set up Socialist Action in 1985. I became a leader of this group and the editor of its magazine.

Socialist Action started with about 25 members, nearly half of whom were in Melbourne. Both Melbourne and Sydney branches were mostly older members, who were pretty much overwhelmed by trying to start over again. Both branches also had little campus work, which made growth difficult. Our most successful branches were in Canberra and Brisbane. In both cases, initially small forces were able to recruit. Rick Kuhn in Canberra gained members from the ANU, from the public service and Women Against Racism.

Carole Ferrier led in Brisbane and recruited at University of Queensland. I remember Carole as someone who hurled herself against the machine. She didn't easily fit into the orthodox machinery of a political organisation. But in the 1970s and 80s when we were carving out our place in the political scene, Carole was an important part of that.

Although our hopes for recruitment centred largely on the campuses, we saw involvement in major class struggles as an essential way for Marxists to remain in touch with the labour movement.

One focus was the Builders Labourers Federation's battle to survive after deregistration in 1986. Most of the far left took up this struggle. We in Socialist Action put more effort into it than just about

BLF SOLIDARITY TICKET
Name: Number: 106
DARE TO STRUGGLE
DARE TO WIN
DEFEND THE UNIONS —
DEFEND THE BLF COMMITTEE.

11
LYGON ST.

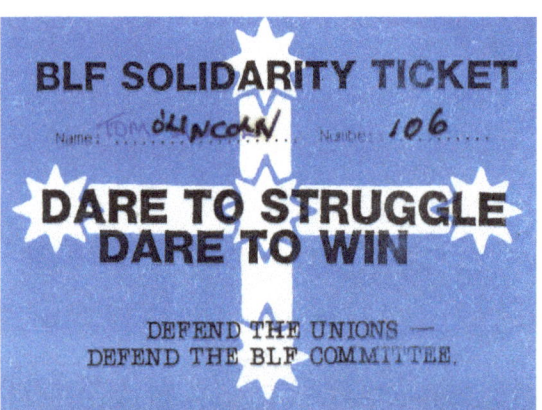

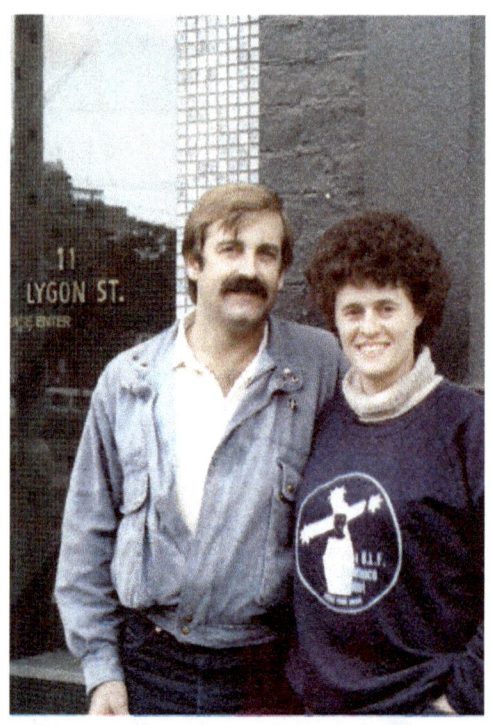

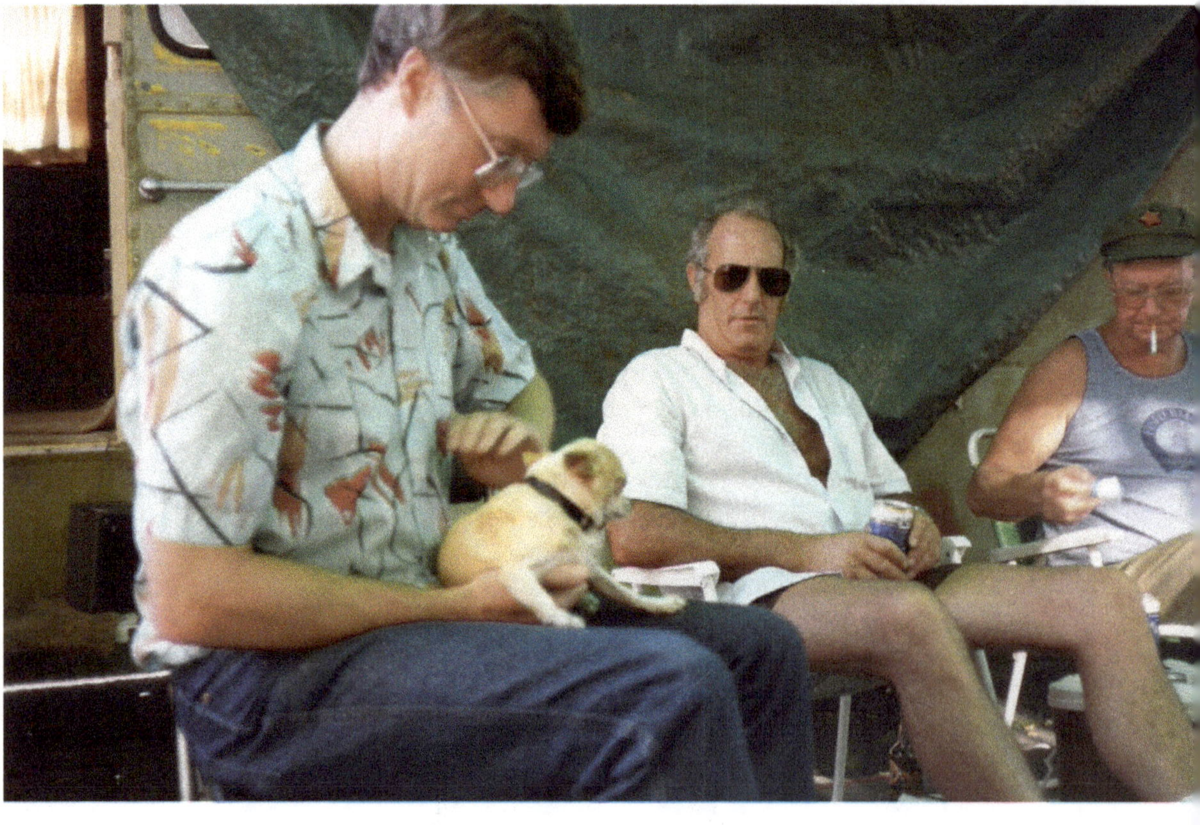

Clockwise from top: SA lining up as part of the BLF contingent Melbourne Mayday, 1986. Chris Clifford in checked shirt, Liz Ross with magazines, Helen Rosenberg with red trousers, David Lockwood visible just past her; BLF picket at Como building site April, 1986 with Liz Ross and Mark Matcott; Chirs Clifford, unknown, and Liz Ross; Tom at brewery drivers' picket in Melbourne, 1987; Tom's BLF solidarity card; Janey with Graeme Haynes outside Melbourne's BLF office. Graeme was touring the country to raise support for Robe River (WA) workers on strike

Clockwise from top: SA weekend school around 1987, (left to right) Rick Kuhn, John Passant, David Lockwood (speaking), Tom (with back to camera), Carole Ferrier, Graham Willett, Jeff Goldhar, Liz Ross; Tom at Socialist Action conference; Mark Harrison, Robert Stainsby, Liz Ross, Chris Clifford, Tony Dewberry (not a member of SA) leaning against the wall

anybody else. Too much perhaps, given the lack of organisational gains we could make. Nonetheless, in Melbourne especially, this campaign kept us in continuing dialogue with a layer of industrial militants and radical activists. Liz Ross's book *Dare to Struggle, Dare to Win!* describes the campaign.

Other activities included the 1988 Melbourne brewery drivers' strike, and the 1988 Robe River (Pilbara, WA) strike, which generated much support activity through the trade union movement nationally. SA was also quite active around the struggle against apartheid in South Africa, and in solidarity with the protesters at Tiananmen Square in 1989. *Socialist Action* magazine, produced monthly, provided a medium for discussion of a wide range of theoretical and contemporary topics.

David Lockwood played a major role in the faction fight and subsequently in Socialist Action. David believed that it was important to challenge dogmatic ideas. At the 1984 Conference at which the faction fight occurred, he did a talk on Victor Serge. We were all pretty much in agreement on what we thought about Victor Serge. But David chose that topic so as to make an argument about standing up against wrong ideas. In that context, it was somewhat provocative.

In the public service, David was an impressive trade unionist. He played a most important role in our work there, along with Liz Ross and Graham Willett. He gave an amazing speech at a public service meeting in Melbourne where we won the vote but knew we would lose it state-wide. He told workers that despite the great vote here, we were going to lose it overall, and the urgent task was to go back to our individual workplaces and fight even harder. He was certainly the left's most talented orator. He would have audiences in stitches, and then in tears.

David fought the organisational battles at a cost to himself. He wasn't always appreciated by the organisations of which he was a member, although he was appreciated.

We were able to continue our direct involvement in trade union activity where we had members, most notably among teachers and in the public service. Socialist Action members played a leading role in the historic strike in the Department of Social Security in Sydney in 1988.

Although I never led a strike, I did acquire personal experience in public service trade unionism. In 1985, after being a full-time socialist activist for nearly 10 years, I started working in

John Passant and Jeff Goldhar; Accord pamphlet produced by SA, written by Liz Ross, Tom O'Lincoln and Graham Willett; Rick Kuhn, Louise Walker and Tom; Eric Petersen

the Commonwealth Public Service.

Here I connected with the generation who had established the ACOA Reform Group, militants like Peter Ellett. It was a well-trodden route. Also, having been in the IS, I already had a feel for work in the public service because quite a lot of our members were working there.

I became a union delegate in my office. It had little impact on the organisation but it did affect me. One quite difficult and controversial trade union case I dealt with concerned someone in my office who was on probation for a criminal conviction. To my surprise, the workers in the office were quite accepting of him – they thought his record was irrelevant to his suitability for employment. I had very little experience but had to go into bat for this guy. I called for assistance from the union and to my amazement, again, the union official, Sue Mountford, came down to back me up and we saved his job, which I probably could not have done on my own.

It is so often the case that a socialist in the workplace will know when to bring in the union. In the end we won, primarily because the officials know what the employer can and cannot get away with.

Later I revisited my old workplace and found that the guy had been elected by his workmates as their union delegate; he seems to have been quite successful in recruiting people to the union.

I began to play more of a role as I gained knowledge and experience. For example, we became aware of how our union officials were selling us out. We began to analyse their wage claims carefully and discovered that they often led to real wage falls rather than rises. I remember one time a very prominent national

182 I.S. in Australia: Socialist Action 1985-89

industrial figure in the union movement came to a meeting to promote enterprise bargaining. We managed to critique, in quite a sophisticated manner, all the arguments the union officials would use to sell us out. For example, they would say the wage claim was indexed to inflation, but we showed that in fact there would be a reduction of wages.

One of the determining features of my work in the public service was the ALP/ACTU Accord, a "social contract" between unions and the government heralded by the incoming Hawke-Keating-led Labor Party in 1983 as bringing a new period of industrial peace and benefits for both workers and employers. Endorsed by most in the trade union movement, including the ACOA, it was heavily criticised by some unions and political groups due to its clear class-collaborationist nature. Unions were to be hobbled by no-strike agreements, two unions were smashed and workers' wages and conditions fell.

The Accord involved a number of stages, each of which included a wage and conditions package which union members had to ratify. By the last years the wage system had shifted from a centralised system to one where workers bargained on a workplace basis for an Enterprise Bargaining Agreement (EBA). In this way Australian capitalism joined the global trend to neoliberalism via another route.

In the federal public sector, union members in most states voted overwhelmingly in favour of endorsing this new system. In Victoria however there was a militant current and it was the state where the most union opposition to the Accord had occurred. We expected the left would put up a good fight, but we were very surprised when public service workers in Melbourne actually voted down the EBA. I remember how Peter Robson, the national secretary of the ACOA, reacted to the defeat. He simply walked out, looking perhaps a bit dismal as the vote went down. Of course we still lost the vote

183   I.S. in Australia: Socialist Action 1985-89

Tom, Helen Rosenberg, Liz Ross, Graham Willett, 1980s

nationally, but it was a good result for the militants here.

Afterwards, Griff rang me asking "What happened at the meeting?" and I said, "Well we won the vote". You could virtually hear his jaw drop.

Despite the difficulties of starting anew in the midst of the 1980s downturn, Socialist Action not only survived but achieved some growth in its nearly five years of separate existence. The IS had a major recruiting boom in 1986 but then lost a lot of ground in the internal crisis that followed, so that both groups had similar rates of growth overall.

Were we right to split from the IS at the time? I think we were right, because sometimes you just have to lay down tracks. When you feel your principles are at stake, it may be necessary to part company. We held a certain group of people together, and we were the first to point to problems which later became evident to everyone.

Through most of the time we were in Socialist Action, the IS was operating with a "gung-ho" approach, riven by its chronic impatience. National Executive members later admitted that the organisation's internal life "closely resembled that of various sects" and that "opposition was generally driven underground", based on the argument that members developed partly through "isolating critics".

Finally in January 1989, the IS conference repudiated the "gung ho" approach, and Socialist Action and the International Socialists fused to form a new organisation called the International Socialist Organisation.

MAY DAY: PHILIPPINES 1987

After the dictatorship of Ferdinand Marcos in the Philippines had fallen in 1986, Liz Ross and I visited the new democracy in May 1987.

In Manila, we attended two very different rallies. On May Day over 100,000 marched under red flags. Nine day later some 30,000 flocked to the final rally for President Cory Aquino's Senate candidates.

The May Day march was spirited, despite 40 degree heat. Vast numbers of young workers, including tens of thousands of women, poured through town, sporting t-shirts emblazoned with the name of the Kilusong Mayu Uno (KMU) union movement. There were also large contingents from all the different factories. The march culminated in a rally where speakers tackled issues like poverty, unemployment and the right to strike. Aquino's labour minister was booed.

By contrast the Aquino election meeting was a superficial affair. Speakers divided their time between phrases about everyone "working together" and attacks on yesterday's tyrant, Ferdinand Marcos. While we had been spared the song and dance acts the candidates had been offering provincial audiences, there was no hint of actual policies.

May Day showed what a powerful movement the Filipino left had built in the factories and poor neighbourhoods. Yet election day showed that capital had an iron grip on the electoral system. Left candidates from the Partigo ng Bayan (PnB – People's Party) got nowhere near being elected into the Senate.

Workers and peasants, who will often accept the leadership of militants in day to day struggle, clearly still had some faith in Aquino when it came to national politics, and her electoral machine delivered an overwhelming win.

Founded in 1980 with 50,000 members, the KMU now represented 700,000 of the two million unionised workers. It competed for influence with the pro-employer yellow unions. It was a young movement and a determined one. After visiting picket lines in Manila and the provinces, we came away with the feeling the KMU took the struggle very seriously. At Globe Steel in East Rizal, we met workers who had been on strike for three years. They now lived in shanties on the picket line. But they also told stories of other local strikers who had won quickly because they had KMU support.

Allied to the KMU were the organisations of the urban poor. We visited the Novotas slum area, where tireless activists moved around the neighbourhood building solidarity where there would otherwise be only despair. The right wing resorted to murder in attempts to intimidate them: the local Navotas leader was gunned down in the street a week before our visit.

The grassroots organisations of the workers and the urban poor were matched by the peasant movement Kilusang Magbubukid ng Pilipinas (KMP – Peasant Movement of the

Philippines). Then there were the "cause-oriented" groups like No Nukes, radical Christians, and the struggles for autonomy among the Muslims of the south and the mountain people of the north. The guerrilla forces of the New People's Army enjoyed widespread sympathy in the provinces – so much so that the government encouraged semi-fascist vigilante groups to counter them.

All these movements faced growing repression from the same government that claimed to be renewing democracy. "Progress under Aquino?" snorted one union activist in Bataan, "Of course. Under Marcos we only had killings. Now we have massacres." So true: troops fired on two hundred workers at the Bataan Export Processing Zone in January 1987, not long before we were there, and killed two. Nine days earlier, 18 peasants had been killed outside the presidential palace in Manila.

With the masses increasingly organised and combative, and the government showing it could be as repressive as Marcos, the opportunity should have been there for a left electoral force to do well. Or so it must have seemed when the Partido ng Bayan was formed.

The left's electoral failure needs some explanation. It was not enough to point to repression and dirty tricks, as the KMU did in a full page advertisement on election day. Certainly the repression was fierce, with 27 left activists being killed. At least 2,837 families were dislocated and thus disenfranchised by conveniently timed military operations. And there was certainly vote-buying and ballot-rigging against right and left wing oppositions. Filipino elections are a rough business, and Aquino fought to win.

The repression and the fraud were to be expected. Yet even well into the campaign, the PnB was confidently expecting to have several senators elected. Some spoke of winning 20 percent of the vote and electing all seven of their candidates. These

A KMU flyer;
(opposite page)
Liz Ross at May
Day in Manila

May Day in Manila; (opposite page) militant striking women workers at Globe Steel, East Rizal

hopes proved unrealistic and it seems clear the PnB underestimated the extent to which the capitalist electoral process always favours the status quo. There are several aspects to this.

To begin with, there is the power of money and institutions. A single 30-second TV ad cost $3-4000, and the country's highest circulation newspaper charged twice that for a full page advertisement. By contrast, Aquino's final election rally was broadcast on TV – all four hours of it.

A range of conservative institutions weighed in on the side of traditional politics. Most notably, the Catholic church described PnB candidates as "lepers". In the localities, Aquino had the services of politically appointed government officials, the Officers-in-Charge who campaigned full time for her candidates. "The OICs have delivered," she remarked on hearing the poll results.

Most of the traditional ruling class clans had regrouped under the Aquino banner, and these still possessed formidable local patronage networks.

Just as important was the ideological aspect. Even in an impoverished and unstable country, capitalism doesn't rule primarily by force. Instead many of the experiences of daily life – the media, Sunday mass, popular jokes and also the complete lack of power that people so often feel – breed a conservative mentality. Capitalism mainly rules with "the consent of the governed" and most elections demonstrate that fact.

As part of a special trade union organised trip, where we visited workplaces, including a mine and community groups, we also went to Smokey Mountain, where 5,000 people live atop and around a gigantic rubbish tip. The place is enveloped in smoke from the spontaneous combustion of organic garbage. Illness and malnutrition are rife.

After Marcos fell, activists moved to strengthen their organisation here, but ran into some resistance. Local people were influenced by charges that the activists were "communists". Although of course the residents of Smokey Mountain have little to fear from communism of whatever brand, they think they do.

A different but related case was the membership of the left's mass organisations. PnB expectations of a big vote relied on adding up the total number of these members, and arriving at several millions. These would get their members to vote PnB, and the left would have the numbers. In fact the left vote didn't reflect these calculations.

This came as a surprise to the activists – but it shouldn't have. Consider how Australian trade unionists once elected communist union leaders to run unions but seldom put them in parliament. There is a gulf for some worker militants between trade union consciousness and political awareness. KMU members were courageous and thoughtful people, but clearly still had illusions in Aquino.

In itself, this was not grounds for us as visitors to despair. We knew that there was still a lot of ferment going on at the time of our visit. In struggle people's ideas can change fast. Just as the apolitical worker of only a few years ago could became the KMU fighter of yesterday, so he or she can learn tomorrow through experience what's wrong with Aquino's government.

That's why the politics of May Day mattered more than election day.

MARKET SOCIALISM IN POLAND AND RUSSIA 1989

Solidarity poster in Poland

In the late 1980s, change was sweeping through the old Soviet bloc. Many groups on the Australian left believed that that the state would transform itself and lead the Soviet Union and the Eastern bloc countries such as Poland and East Germany in a healthy direction.

In fact, it soon became clear the direction was a restructuring of plain old capitalism, with democratic change limited to elections. Even so there were lessons for socialists. Andrei Sakharov was still putting his heart and soul into the reform movement known as *glasnost*, or transparency. A miners' strike shook Soviet society, but there were far too few revolutionaries to give it direction. Upon the death of Andrei Sakharov, *Pravda* featured a poem beginning: "His heart went on strike like a coal mine". It was far too late.

Poland – Stalinism at the crossroads

In this environment we wanted to take a first-hand look at the emerging "market socialism", so in 1989 Liz Ross and I travelled to the region. We went to Poland first, where things had developed a long way. *Solidarnosc* (Solidarity) had taken power after mass uprisings by workers during 1988 and 1989 which had forced the Jaruzelski government to concede limited elections and legalisation of the union.

Jozef Pinior was the treasurer of the original *Solidarnosc* movement founded in September 1980 at the Lenin Shipyards in Gdansk under Lech Walesa. When the government cracked down in 1981, many activists got caught with whatever they had on them at the time. But Pinior managed to escape with all the union funds. His escape meant that *Solidarnosc* had sufficient funds to continue to function for a considerable period of time underground. Pinior was quite politically adept and also politically clear on a number of issues. At the time that we were there, Pinior and a number of others had left Solidarity and formed the Polish Socialist Party (PPS). They then had another split to form the PPS-RD (Democratic Revolution), which was a group closer to our politics, in the sense of trying to break with the system. Pinior was one of the founders of both of these parties.

For these reasons we wanted to talk to him about contemporary politics in Poland. We were lucky enough to be able to set up a meeting with him in Wroclaw. Pinior and his comrades were in the process of clarifying their positions, so we chose to focus

Liz Ross with Jozef Pinior in Poland; (opposite page) Tom outside of the Winter Palace in Petrograd, Russia

on the theory of state capitalism, which he and his political supporters found interesting.

Pinior said, "Stalinism is at the crossroads. Everyone in the opposition movements agrees that we must overthrow it. For this, international links are essential, including links with groups in Russia. You cannot have socialism in one country. The aim is to build through the Eastern bloc for a party."

We put the question of what a Solidarity government meant to PPS-RD members. Liz summarised their reply in her article in *Socialist Action* magazine.

> The party argues that the new government is an improvement on the Jaruzelski regime – almost anything would be – but that the free market solutions to the crisis being advanced by both Solidarity and the PUWP are not in the workers' interests. For example, most of the food queues have disappeared. But that is only because the price reform has meant that many people can't afford to buy what's in the shops. The PPS-RD argues for direct links between the Solidarity rank and file and the farmers, instead of ending subsidies and allowing the market to decide.[24]

We also spoke to some steel workers in Wroclaw who were active in Solidarity, which was not just a mass movement, but was also the union that covered workers in most workplaces. We talked about their workplace and the more general political situation within Solidarity and Poland itself. They had quite developed critiques of Solidarity and ideas about what needed to be done to take the struggle forward.

Another important struggle in Poland was over abortion, which had previously been freely available. In 1989 the Catholic church moved to limit abortions and while Solidarity's leader Lech Walesa agreed to it, there was fierce opposition from most Poles. In Bydgoszcz a group of Solidarity factory activists gathered signatures to a petition and claimed that Solidarity leadership was "too much in the hands of the church". Mass demonstrations in May 1989 forced the government to back down, but activists warned that further struggles would be needed.

Dissidents in Russia

From Poland we moved on to the Soviet Union, where the situation was more contradictory. We attended a rally where one speaker was Andrei Sakharov, a nuclear scientist who had been a very prominent figure. Then he decided he didn't approve of the way nuclear science was being used by the rulers of the Soviet Union. He became the best known dissident in Russia.

At the time, the two terms that everyone was talking about with reference to Russia were *glasnost* and *perestroika*. These are not actually very significant terms in Russian: *glasnost* means "transparency" and *perestroika* means "restructuring". The words were used in the Soviet Union in much the same way such words are used here by management consultants. But in the West they gained a seemingly magical quality.

In practice, they didn't lead to radical change. They led to what we've got today, Vladimir Putin – not exactly what people were looking for!

At the time of our visit, this was not resolved. The question still was: where is this society heading? One of the things that we saw very clearly was that the place was collapsing, that it was not able to sustain its position in the world using the model of development it had used since the 1930s.

There were Trotskyists in Russia and we met Sergei, who published Trotsky's *Permanent Revolution* in Russian. But apart from him and a

few older Trotskyists there were no organised Trotskyist groups. This was because of Stalin's persecution of dissidents, but it seemed the political upheavals had not (yet) encouraged more to turn to Trotsky's analysis.

Boris Kagarlitsky, a famous dissident in the Soviet Union, was in London to receive the Deutscher Prize, so we did not get to meet him.

There were two main dissident currents at the time. Kagarlitsky's grouping, the Moscow People's Front, was sophisticated in terms of social analysis but not really thoroughly revolutionary in my opinion – not sufficiently militant. The Democratic Union was more militant and more sharply hostile to the regime, but did not have the richness of social analysis that Kagarlitsky was able to provide. The two needed to come together in some way, but that never happened.

Out on the Moscow street was another reality from the political argumentation. Food shops with nothing but giant pickled onions, and Pepsi machines that did not, anywhere, seem to work. Administration that owed much to Franz Kafka. A political system pointing to Boris Yeltsin.

One crucial question for us was the situation of women. It is a convention on the left, and was a truism in the USSR itself, that women there were equal to men. We wanted to gain material that would help us to counter this view. Some feminists use

Tom with a group of Kagarlitsky supporters; (opposite page) Tom at dinner with Russian activists after the Sakharov rally

the continuing existence of sexism to argue that we'll need another "women's revolution" after a socialist revolution. With our analysis that the societies of the Soviet bloc were not socialist but state capitalist, we would expect women were still oppressed there, as in all class societies.

One example of supposed evidence of equality given was the large number of women construction engineers. We visited a female construction engineer and it was clear that their position in society was not fundamentally different to what it was in the West.

We interviewed Olga Lipovskaya, editor of the Leningrad *samizdat* journal *Women's Reading*. Liz and I reported in *Socialist Action* in 1989:

> She told us, "women are now being blamed for all the problems of the family (and) for the plight of abandoned children", which in turn leads to propagating the idea that "women should stay in the home". This has much to do with economic restructuring, for in cases where enterprises lay off workers, "of course it will be women who lose their jobs".

195 Market socialism in Poland and Russia 1989

Tom in front of Lenin's tomb, Red Square, Moscow

Answers from a historian

One issue I've addressed often is the nature of the Soviet Union and similar societies. Were they really socialist? Debate broke out in the Soviet Union itself in 1988-89 over just this question. An intellectual named Yuri Afanasiev published a piece in 1988 entitled "Perestroika and Historical Knowledge". In it Afanasiev raised the question as to whether there could have been an alternative to the path followed by Stalin in his drive to industrialise Russia, and implied that the gradual approach favoured by Nikolai Bukharin in the late thirties would have been preferable.

Afanasiev raised so much interest that he was attacked in *Pravda*. The idea was to intimidate him – and this came from the top. He responded to the attacks with an article entitled "Answers from a historian", in which he wrote:

> I do not consider the society created in our country to be socialist, not even a deformed socialism. These deformations concern its vital foundations, political system, relations of production and all the rest.[25]

You could see this was someone who was critical of the *regime*, but was not critical of *socialism*; he actually had a tremendous *desire* for socialism. He just thought you have to start with the facts.

I was very interested in Afanasiev's article, and ended up brushing up my Russian and making my own translation, recently published in my book *"The expropriators are expropriated" and other writings on Marxism.* I found his concluding paragraphs in particular very moving:

> A lot has changed in the last three years, and we are full of hope. Hope for socialism. Hope of liberated labour, prosperity, democracy.
>
> And the questions to historians, and to politicians – ah, how many there are. And the answers are varied and controversial. However I think there is something that shouldn't be controversial. Was that socialism we have had, or "barracks socialism"? ("On the one hand" the jar is half full of honey, "on the other hand" it is half full of tar)?
>
> We'll see the answer in five or ten years. Either we become a completely different country, an unrecognizably different and flourishing society, or we continue with the profound discussions about the famous "inconsistencies" of a socialism without freedom and without bread and butter. Only how much more time will history allow us for this entrancing casuistry?
>
> If the idea of socialism, after all we've lived through, is still clear and dear to us, then dear comrades, let us dust it off and save it up for a better future. It might come in handy.

AN INSPIRING REVOLUTIONARY: SOUTH KOREA 1991

In 1991, I visited South Korea with Liz Ross. South Korea has a long history of repression but also a history of inspiring fightbacks. One of the first things we did in Seoul was to visit the strike at Westpac strike, an industrial dispute which we'd heard about before we departed.

We were able to directly interact with the workers: management walked out as soon as we appeared. The first thing they did as soon as they had the place to themselves was to unfold their banners and launch into songs and chants. This demonstrated one of their tactics, an alternative to going out on strike. Sometimes they march around the workplace banging drums loudly and making it impossible for people to keep on working.

The strikers later came to

KOREAN PUBLISHER JAILED

Free Il-bung Choi

ON Thursday 7 January, Il-bung Choi, a Korean socialist, was sentenced to two years' imprisonment. His crime? Publishing books—books which are freely available in western countries.

The prosecution was carried out under the McCarthyite National Security Law, which restricts civil liberties using the "threat from the north" as the excuse.

But the books for which Il-bung Choi is being jailed are just as opposed to the undemocratic system of North Korea as they are to that of the South.

In his speech to the court, Il-bung Choi declared that he was a socialist and a Marxist, but denied that this reflected influence from the north. He told how he had been a Christian interested in liberation theology who had become a Marxist through the study of society, of history and philosophy.

INSPIRED

He told how he had been inspired by the history of people's self-emancipation, from the slave revolt led by Spartacus through to the 1987 workers' revolt in South Korea itself. Even

authorised visit to North Korea and his secretary Pang Yang-kyun who was sentenced for seven years for failing to report the visit and allegedly passing on state secrets. Both men were tortured during interrogation.

Amnesty International has documented numerous accounts of torture and ill-treatment of political prisoners, including prisoners being beaten and deprived of sleep during interrogation.

REFORMS

The election, in December, of Kim Young Sam as President of South Korea was widely hailed in the west as heralding new democratic reforms. He is a former oppositionist and the first civilian president since the military seized power in 1960.

Yet even as Kim Young Sam was campaigning as the representative of the ruling party, Il-bung Choi was being prosecuted in court.

His case is a serious test of whether the regime's reforms mean anything; whether the rulers of South Korea will tolerate dissent.

In London, a number of well-known figures have signed a letter of protest against the jailing of Il-bung Choi. They include MPs Tony Benn

Melbourne after we returned, and we organised a demonstration in Collins Street, outside the Westpac Bank – we were glad to have this opportunity to show solidarity to workers whose picket line we'd visited in South Korea. Just as at home, they unfurled banners and launched into songs and chants.

Eventually, after a record 124 days, Westpac closed down the Seoul branch. They refused to agree

Clockwise from left: Tom interviewing a Westpac striker; *The Australian* 7 January 1991; Westpac strikers; (opposite page) ISO support leaflet following arrest of Il Bung Choi

Liz Ross with Il Bung Choi

a small but seemingly very good group of 20. They are publishing an article of mine in their mag so they must be good…

Our main contact in this group was Il Bung Choi, a very inspiring revolutionary. He began to develop revolutionary politics while he was a student in the US. Returning to Korea he was instrumental in setting up what was, at the time we were there, a significant left group. One thing that really struck me about him was his enormous capacity to withstand imprisonment. I found the idea of being stuck in a Korean prison somewhat daunting, but it didn't seem to faze him at all.

When Il Bung Choi was again imprisoned shortly after we left South Korea, we demonstrated at the World Trade Centre in Melbourne.

The visit to Korea also taught us a little about organising politically in a repressive state. We were invited to attend a meeting. We joined several people in a car and set out for this meeting. We didn't realise that they had to make a phone call first, followed up by several more as we drove from point to point through Seoul, to find out where the meeting was. They had to maintain this security to avoid arrest. But they managed it.

to the union demand that it be part of an advisory committee on redundancies and other relevant matters. The bosses were making a statement about their absolute right to control the workplace. They were prepared to grant some wage rises which the workers were asking for, but certainly not prepared to cede any effective control.

We also met up with the local International Socialist Tendency group in Seoul. In a postcard to Janey I wrote:

> Only a day here and we're straight into the politics… [We encountered]

I.S. IN AUSTRALIA: THE 1990s

Socialist Action and the International Socialists fused to form the International Socialist Organisation in 1989. Although there were some tensions, unity did create a new hope. At least we did not have to compete on the basis of very similar politics.

Our reunified organisation was established just in time to greet world-historic events.

The 1980s ended with the collapse of Eastern Europe's Stalinist dictatorships, symbolised by the fall of the Berlin Wall. For us it was a vindication; our next national event featured a huge banner inscribed with Trotsky's words: "The vengeance of history is more terrible than the vengeance of the most powerful General Secretary".

Having analysed the Eastern bloc as a kind of capitalism system, we weren't demoralised when the workers tore it down. This did raise theoretical issues, though. We didn't see it as a historic step backwards, but neither was it a historic step forwards, given that the introduction of the free market would now bring its own version of capitalist misery. Also we were far from clear on how unified the global economy and political system was. We expected the crisis in the state capitalist society to flow on to a crisis everywhere else.

And in some ways it seemed to. The collapse of Soviet power left a geopolitical vacuum, which America's first Bush administration filled by waging war on Iraq. Around the same time, Western economies fell into a sharp recession. In Victoria, Jeff Kennett led the Liberals to a landslide

(NAME)

Tom O'Lincoln

is a member of the

Melbourne North

branch of the
International Socialist Organisation

'Only the working class has the power to create a society free from exploitation, oppression and want.

'... Crucial to a workers' movement smashing the capitalist state is a revolutionary workers' party built out of the day to day struggle...'

ISO - 'What We Stand For'

NAME:

ADDRESS:

PHONE:

UNION/CAMPUS:

electoral victory over a discredited ALP administration in 1992, and immediately slashed public sector jobs as well as attacking union rights. The unions fought back with huge demonstrations.

At the time of its creation, the ISO still assumed downturn conditions would continue, and so it identified itself as a propaganda group. But on the basis of international events, by 1992 the International Socialist Tendency was concluding that things were getting a lot better for socialists.

And yes, the ISO did well in the early nineties, growing from 150 members in 1990 to 250 in 1993. The group threw itself into protest actions in 1991 against a visit by George Bush Snr and against the AIDEX arms fair. At the same time it published six issues of a theoretical journal. These two facts go some distance to summarising the strengths of the group at that time: combining dramatic interventions in struggle with an ambitious program of self-education.

The growth wasn't just numerical. In the early 1990s, the ISO had a substantial body of older members with considerable sophistication; not only in theoretical terms but also in terms of practical politics, because we had been through such chastening experiences. This along with the militant interventions attracted serious fighters.

Yet the growth stalled by 1993, just as we adopted an overly ambitious new perspective based on an overestimation of the political situation. Western capitalism displayed more stability than we had expected. A confused conflict broke out in the IS leadership, born of frustration at our lack of progress, and it spread throughout the organisation. In 1995 a new split tore the ISO apart.

Tom singing *The Internationale* at fusion of IS and SA to form ISO in 1989; (opposite page) Tom's ISO membership card

I stepped down from the ISO National Committee in 1992. Twenty years of leadership had taken its toll. I decided that I was not temperamentally suited to being on national executive bodies. I stepped down from them permanently. I therefore participated in the factional conflicts of the 1990s as a rank and file member.

From 1993, the leadership argued that there had been a massive increase in the opportunities to build a revolutionary socialist organisation. Anyone who doubted that was a conservative element, "stuck in the eighties". On the basis of this over-optimistic assessment the leadership promised dramatic growth, time and again. Time and again they failed to deliver. The result was a long and destructive internal conflict, culminating in the split that created Socialist Alternative.

I stayed on in the ISO after a large section of the Melbourne membership was expelled, going on to form Socialist Alternative (SAlt) in 1995. Apart from its small size, it seemed to me that SAlt in its early days lacked political clarity.

After the split, the ISO for a time did not implement the more extreme elements of their perspective, partly because they had been weakened by the split. One result was that the Melbourne branches did quite well, they grew, and things looked hopeful for a few years. But as soon as the organisation started to look healthy and solid, the leadership moved to reintroduce all the organisational restructures that had wrecked it before.

By 1999, the ISO had entered a fantasy world of mass campaigning – what I called a "one-legged perspective". The adoption of an "Action Program", a concept borrowed from the British Socialist Workers Party, was an attempt to present demands for the rest of the movements; and something the group could mobilise around on a mass basis. Formulated for a completely different political situation, it had little relevance and no chance of winning support.

At the time, the dominant political issue was the invasion of East Timor by the Australian army. It had widespread support, even among the left, with the ISO and Socialist Alternative the only groups protesting the army's actions. It was a time to be discussing Australian imperialism, not a concocted Action Program.

The ISO seemed to be unable to develop a strategy based on conditions in Australia. I could see trouble coming again.

A similar situation came in the wake of the large and significant S11 protest in 2000. Like all the left, the ISO grew, but in numbers too big for the group to manage, and on a flimsy political basis. Claiming a membership in the hundreds, while the real membership was in the tens, seriously disoriented the group, leading to more tensions.

This demonstrated to me that the ISO had not overcome its ultra-left ideas, its impatience. I wrote in an internal document in 2002:

> A small group needs to combine limited practical priorities with a very wide horizon of ideas. Lenin's 1917 Bolsheviks intervened in every sphere of society, pulling things together while at the same time they hammered three simple slogans: peace, bread and land. On the other hand we need to concentrate on a few areas of (practical) work, while developing propaganda about the widest possible intellectual universe.
>
> If we try to prioritise every area of practical work we will end up with no real priorities. We'll race around from one thing to another, with diminishing resources as people start to burn out.

I argued that we were a propaganda group and that you can't break out of being a small group by willpower. To no avail. The ISO looked like it was going to destroy itself, which it did do in the end. So in 2002 I resigned.

After a break I joined Socialist Alternative in 2003, although I was still not sure that they had clarified their politics. But I had been impressed by their role in organising the protest against Pauline Hanson at the Hawthorn Town Hall in 1998. Because I knew that being in an organisation was the only way to organise politically, I joined the only viable revolutionary organisation around.

I remain a member. I have never regretted it.

EYEWITNESS TO MASS STRUGGLE: INDONESIA 1993-2001

Pamphlet of a collection of articles from the Indonesian-language email magazine *Suara Sosialis* produced by Tom 1997-2003

In the early 1990s I started on a new project. I was looking for something to do, as I was unhappy with the internal situation the ISO at the time, so I thought I'd learn a new language.

I was visiting my mother every second night at the time. So I got an Indonesian book and studied it on the tram, which gave me a fair amount of time, Brunswick to Caulfield. I would sit there mumbling to myself over the Indonesian book – to the annoyance of the regular passengers who knew the moment they saw me that I was going to start mumbling again.

I started learning in 1993 and spent three years using the book and talking to Indonesians in Melbourne. Indonesian has a very large number of loan words from Dutch, English and other languages. I did not find it too difficult to learn. Things were happening politically in Indonesia and I could follow political developments covered by the *Green Left Weekly*.

Having got oriented, I started going to Indonesia. By this point my language ability was adequate for political discussions – depending on who I was talking to. Gradually my language improved.

Chatting with a police detective in Jakarta

Sukarno, who had been the leader of the independence struggle from the Netherlands, was president of Indonesia from 1945 to 1967. Following a military coup in 1965, at least half a million people were massacred and one and a half million imprisoned, a large number of them Communist Party members and leftists. General Suharto held effective power for 23 years from the coup until his resignation in 1998.

The cracks started to appear in 1994, when Megawati Sukarnoputri, daughter of Sukarno, became leader of the Indonesian Democratic Party (PDI).

On 27 July 1996, gangs backed by Suharto's military attacked the Jakarta offices of the PDI. The dictator had previously arranged a rigged PDI conference to get Megawati dumped as leader, but her supporters had defiantly occupied the headquarters.

The attack provoked mass upheavals usually called the 27 July riots, though they were much more political than most riots, with people marching and chanting slogans. The unrest shocked the regime, which was quick to blame it on an obscure far left group called the People's Democratic Party (PRD), led by Budiman Sudjatmiko.

Three months earlier I'd met with Budiman and his comrades in a shabby little house in the crowded Jakarta district of Tebet. They were still assembling their tiny organisation and preparing a declaration, not dreaming what a storm was about to hit them.

The government's charge that the PRD fomented the riots was idiotic. They were far too small to cause

Demonstrators in 1997 outside the courtroom during sentencing of Budiman and other PRD figures. Photo: Tom O'Lincoln

unrest on the scale of 27 July. But Suharto needed scapegoats.

Budiman and other official PRD leaders went on the run until the cops tracked them down. Others, who had kept a lower profile, maintained an underground organisation that sent me stirring emails – but after the riots things looked pretty grim, with Megawati's movement paralysed and the far left marginalised. The PRD leaders made defiant statements in court and awaited their fate.

In April 1997 I returned to Jakarta. It was election time, but seemingly this meant little. The polls were rigged at the best of times – all the more so now with a Suharto stooge leading the PDI, and the Muslim-based PPP (*Partai Persatuan Pembangunan*, Development Unity Party) unwilling to challenge the regime.

We heard they were sentencing Budiman and other PRD figures, so our destination was Central Jakarta Court. Arriving early, I sat on a bench outside and fell into a conversation with a pleasant man. What was I doing here? Oh, I was here to see the sentencing. Why my interest in that? Oh,

207   Eyewitness to mass struggle: Indonesia

I had met Budiman before. I vaguely realised I was name-dropping, boasting about knowing Budiman, so I changed the topic, asking about the pleasant man's background. "Oh, I'm a police detective."

There I sat, feeling idiotic and scared at the same time.

But he wandered off harmlessly, so I went into the packed courtroom, where attendance was a political statement. We heard muffled shouting when the prisoners arrived, then they stamped up the stairs yelling "*Boikot pemilu!*" (Boycott the elections!). The media rushed about; the crowd cheered; supporters gave the prisoners flowers. Budiman made a fiery declaration, and they sentenced him to 13 years.

Suharto's fall would get him out much sooner, but at the time it seemed terrible. A few people drifted outside, where a token demonstration on the sidewalk faced aggressive cops who kept pushing the protesters back. Then suddenly the demonstrators turned and charged onto the road, setting off with banners in an illegal street march. The flabbergasted police stumbled after them.

The elections themselves proved more interesting than expected. The regime allowed a "festival of democracy", with not only political rallies but above all the *arak-arakan*, massive motorcades around city streets. Macho young men gunned their motorbikes, people piled on top of trucks, everyone wore party colours. I couldn't believe how big the PPP motorcades were getting. Was this normal? No, something important was happening. With Megawati sidelined, support for the PDI had collapsed, while everyone despised Suharto's ruling Golkar organisation. So the PPP became the focus of opposition despite its tame-cat leaders. For once this useless party attracted huge crowds, in an amazing phenomenon called Mega-Star.

Mega was short for Megawati, the star was the PPP symbol and Megawati's angry supporters joined the PPP rallies in a massive show of opposition to the regime. The city ground to a halt. Twice I travelled across a capital city whose major roads were gridlocked for hours. Where buses got stuck in traffic, people danced on the roof. It all culminated in street fighting. This was a confused but real uprising of the masses, and somewhere out there among them, the PRD was doing its best to hammer home a third and more radical dimension, with the slogan *Mega-Bintang-Rakyat* (Mega-Star-The People).

The Suara Sosialis project

Back home, in 1997 I began an Indonesian-language email magazine called *Suara Sosialis* (Socialist Voice), which became a six-year project to produce Marxist material in that language. I started sending the newsletter to 20 addresses initially, with mostly English-language material but one item in Indonesian each month. As my language skills got better, I moved to exclusively Indonesian language content. The substantial articles went on a website, step by step. The site promoted the newsletter – classic e-commerce principles at work!

It was the first-ever Marxist website in the Indonesian language.

I could never have done this without help from an Indonesian comrade, Setiabudi, who lived in Melbourne and who cleaned up the texts in the way only a native speaker can do.

The first articles were a popular "What is Socialism?" series. After that we moved to more substantial material, most importantly translating John Molyneux's *What is the Real Marxist Tradition*? The plan was to work through all the key theoretical issues. Eventually there were all sorts of topics covered on the site, from "Marxism and Religion" to "Discussion of Homosexuality".

Subscribers multiplied, till the

John Molyneux's *What is the real Marxist tradition* translated into Indonesian by Tom and Setiabudi

list reached about 250. We also participated in a project putting the first Indonesian-language versions of key documents onto the web, including the *Communist Manifesto* and Lenin's *April Theses*.

Each year, I went off to Indonesia with a new set of material, tightly laid out and laser-printed so that activists there could photocopy the texts as much as possible from the copies I provided. Thinking the Suharto regime might take an undesired interest in me, I used the pseudonym "Julian". The name stuck, and that Julian guy developed a certain profile around the Indonesian left. His less obscure real-life double spoke at a number of public forums and debates around Java.

In between visits, "Julian" became a fixture on the "Indo-Marxist" e-mail discussion list. One furious debate with Ma'ruf, a leader of the People's Democratic Party (PRD), got wide attention. We canvassed the virtues and sins of Ma'ruf's organisation and mine without kid gloves. As it happened, Ma'ruf soon left the PRD and I later left the ISO, and we have had friendly discussions since.

In the end there were perhaps 100,000 words of Indonesian-language Marxist materials on the *Suara Sosialis* site, and much of it was published in that country, in the form of three books. How many pages of photocopied material got around, we can only speculate.

It was sad to end the project, but by 2003 it had clearly run its course, both for the Indonesians and myself.

The participants had developed new priorities and circumstances had changed. For myself, I had buried myself in Indonesia work partly because I was dissatisfied with my organisation. I figured they wouldn't take much interest in the details of what I did in a foreign country and a foreign language, and that I would have a free hand. But this only worked for so long. After Suharto fell, the British SWP leaders did take an interest and generated what I thought was a mistaken line on the "Indonesian revolution" – which however rapidly became orthodoxy in my own group the Australian ISO. I was discontented again. There was no escape!

Whatever the political and personal implications were, it was better anyway not to get in a rut: the key material we set out to produce was basically complete. On 27 July 2003 I sent off the final edition of the magazine. It was *selamat jalan* (farewell) to the project. But the *perjuangan* (struggle) continued.

Wild in the streets

May 1998 and I was on a visit to Jakarta. Things were hopeful, things were tense. The Asian economic crisis had shattered the Indonesian economy and the capital was a tinderbox. Mass unemployment, student democracy movements, riots, strikes, police violence – you name it, Jakarta had it. Just about everyone thought Suharto's regime had to go, but still he hung on, picking his way through the minefield of an IMF austerity program.

Then one evening we tried to catch a taxi. The simplest thing, yet to our amazement none would stop: they were all heading for petrol stations to get the last drops before the government, under the IMF lash, slashed subsidies. Buses were doing the same. Everybody was looking for the same thing, but some had an easier time getting it.

Rich people sent their drivers to join the queues; then the drivers headed home to empty the tanks before returning to queue again. Meanwhile working class people had to trudge home on foot. Looking helplessly at this orgy of greed, the poorer neighbourhoods seethed with resentment. We should know, we were forced to walk through them for miles.

On 14 May the morning papers told me snipers had shot demonstrating students at the Trisakti campus in West Jakarta. I found a taxi and headed over there, telling the driver I was going to the nearby Citraland hotel and shopping mall – he might have been scared of going to Trisakti. The police were nowhere to be seen; they feared the people's anger.

At the university a rally was

Moreland Sentinal 1 June, 1998. Tom interviewed after his return from Indonesia

underway. For the moment it was peaceful. Megawati arrived, as did rival democracy figure Amien Rais. So did the poet Rendra, who had written verses for the occasion.

Speakers appealed for non-violence, but it was too late for that. Militant students were already drifting into the streets, where they mingled with neighbourhood poor. Student officials tried in vain to stop them. Someone pulled concrete planter boxes into the road and blocked traffic.

I ran into friends from the Women's Solidarity NGO, and we grabbed some lunch from the student canteen while watching the restless crowds in the streets. They said, "This anger has been buried in their hearts for a long time."

Police formed up some distance away, but when they showed no signs of moving, I went out to talk to people in the street. One young guy pointed to the fat, vulgar tower of the Citraland hotel across the road, where the attached shopping mall had slammed its doors shut. "Later we'll burn that down," he said, pulling at the sides of his eyes to signify the owner was Chinese. "Don't be racist." I argued with a boldness I didn't feel. "Suharto's the problem, and he's not Chinese." To my amazement the young man blinked and nodded OK; and I felt like I'd accomplished something. A drop in the ocean. But my drop.

The crowd started to run. My head spinning, I dashed with them back onto the campus. Then looking around, I realised there was no danger yet. I traded glances with the woman next to me. "*Kita panik,*" (We panicked), I said. She nodded and we both laughed.

After a while I went out into the other street around the corner from the campus. Some people had set fire to a truck. No police were around yet so I stopped to photograph it. As I walked back some young guys called out "*Berita hangat*" (Hot news). We laughed and then they asked what I thought. I said to them, "Isn't this rioting dangerous?" "We're just getting started," they replied.

Soon it was on. The students had become more daring, and set fire to a police post, then a petrol station. The demonstrators charged, throwing rocks, in a display of mad courage. The police shot tear gas, scary yet oddly nostalgic; it was the first time I'd smelt that raw, pungent aroma since Berkeley in the sixties. I was inside the now-locked campus gates, watching, and feeling safe – until a gas grenade flew right into the university grounds, and we were all running

news extra
No tears for a fallen leader

Violence in Jakarta may erupt again

MASSIVE civil unrest could erupt again in Indonesia unless the country changed its economic and power structures, a Brunswick resident who witnessed rioting and looting last month has warned.

Tom O'Lincoln said the fall of Soeharto was a great victory. But he said the Indonesians' celebrations could be overrun by the impact of the country's growing economic crisis.

He said the country's unofficial 13 million unemployed were struggling to afford staple foods.

Mr O'Lincoln said he wanted massive redistribution of the state's economy, wealth and power.

Mr O'Lincoln, a member of the International Socialists organisation for 30 years, was in conference with student activists on his third annual trip to Jakarta when riots and looting broke out.

"The problem with a 30-year dictatorship is there are no mechanisms for change," he said.

What's missing is a labor movement. The unions are government run and the independent ones are still pretty weak.

"What's needed is a movement from the working class — some sort of mass movement to give all the people burning down buildings a political alternative.

"The real problem is this: the power of the masses at one level is huge.

NO ARMCHAIR revolutionary, Tom O'Lincoln was among the throng of students who spilled from Trisakti University on to Jakarta's streets during the student uprising.

Known as a campus for "rich" kids whose parents bought them a place on any other day Trisakti University...

Brunswick activist Tom O'Lincoln was in Indonesia when the events that triggered the fall of President Soeharto unfolded. Martine Borrack reports.

Among the speakers on campus, streets too. He became aware of riot...

"As I walked back some young guys called out 'berita hangat', which means 'hot news'. We laughed and then they asked what I thought. I said to them 'Isn't this rioting dangerous?'

"We're just getting started. Later on we're going to burn down Citraland (a giant shopping complex and hotel nearby)," they told him.

again, helter-skelter, choking.

Barging into a building, dashing up the stairs looking for water, I met a lecturer. As we coughed together, she told me her son had lost his job in the economic upheavals, and she might be next. Eventually we cautiously ventured out; she led to me a side gate out of the campus and together we crossed the pedestrian bridge over the freeway to the Citraland side. A cop looked suspiciously at my camera. I pretended to only speak English. "Thank you very much," I said inconsequentially. "Thank you," he mumbled back, not sure what to do except let me pass.

Traffic was jammed tight. A police radio squawked, "The mobile brigade armoured vehicles are caught in traffic." Looking down from the bridge, sure enough I saw them, powerless for once.

All the streets were just as jammed. There was nothing for it but to walk out of the riot zone. I plodded along in the hot, smoggy afternoon. Along the way a street vendor glanced at me, and back at where I'd come from. "*Ramai, pak?*" (Hectic over there?) "*Ramai*", I replied. We laughed. It was going to get a lot more hectic, and within a short time Suharto would be history. Seven days later, after decades in power, Suharto had fallen.

Welcome to the police station

Another visit to Jakarta, June 2001. One steamy Thursday morning we rumbled out of Jakarta on the slowest, oldest rattletrap bus any of us had ever seen. We were headed for an Asia Pacific Solidarity Conference. Few of us knew our exact destination though, because the conference we'd registered for didn't yet have a police permit and security was tight.

It turned out to be a golf club in Sawangan to the south-west. The club was very pleasant indeed. The food was terrific. The first afternoon brought a spectacular and rather beautiful electric storm.

A series of sometimes stormy debates continued into the next day, but the forces of the state kept their distance, and we began to relax a bit about security. Then halfway through Friday I left the auditorium. Before I came back, armed police had arrived from all direction, and a tense confrontation was underway.

The conference still lacked a permit, and the police were saying we 40 or so foreign participants had misused our visas, pretending to be tourists when we were really there for a political event. They demanded we climb onto open trucks. But at the urging of our hosts, we refused.

We sat around the tables; the Indonesian participants clustered around us. When the cops tried to pull us out of the tangle, the organisers argued: "These are foreign citizens, you can't treat them like that." Wide-eyed young cops, used only to mistreating their own citizens, let go of us and the stand-off continued. The Indonesian comrades began singing the left anthem *Darah Juang* (Blood of Struggle).

I knew the chorus but had never sung it in circumstances like these.

> *Mereka dirampas haknya*
> *tergusur dan lapar.*
> *Bunda relakan darah juang kami,*
> *Tuk membebaskan rakyat*
> *Padamu kami berbakti,*
> *Padamu kami mengabdi.*

> Their rights are taken away
> they are evicted and hungry.
> Our mothers are willing for us to shed
> our blood,
> To liberate the people
> To you we are devoted,
> You we serve.[26]

We held out for an hour, before finally climbing onto the trucks which rolled back into Jakarta, sirens blaring. On the streets, people stared at these foreigners assembled on police vehicles. We spent the journey tearing our address books into confetti which blew in our wake. The cops would find no clues. As we began approaching the centre of town, the guy next to me spied a signboard he could half read with his phrase-book: "*Selamat datang* – we're welcome," he laughed. Well might we laugh: the sign said *Selamat Datang di Polda Metro Jaya* (Welcome to the police station).

They took our passports and put us in the Crisis Room – that sign was in English. The authorities had used this place to plan security during massive demonstrations outside the 1998 parliamentary special session. Here we would spend 24 hours. Diplomatic staff started to appear, including a tense man from the Australian consulate who was very, very anxious to get us out of Indonesia – but not, as I first had assumed, because he was concerned for us.

Local and international media began arriving next. Soon our faces popped up on Jakarta TV. The rank and file police in the station were agog – what had they got themselves into? Through our one cell phone held by Belgian comrade Jean Duval, calls came in from around the globe. Protests were underway internationally. Far to the south, true to form, Australia's foreign minister Alexander Downer was backing the cops.

Our leader through most of this was the well-known activist Max Lane. Max had once been cultural counsellor in the Australian embassy, and had the best tactical sense for this situation. He was brilliant. But his high blood pressure began to affect him, and I was asked to take on the negotiating role because it required language skills.

I was just getting my head together to do this when the police brought in

Jakarta Post 12 June, 2001 showing detained westerners, Tom seated centre left

finger-printing gear and cameras. Our Legal Aid lawyers warned this could set a bad precedent, so we refused to be fingerprinted or photographed. The consulate man was beside himself. You have to cooperate, he harangued, the police are within their rights, the stakes are too high. When we stood our ground he looked daggers at the lawyers. What was with this guy, I began to wonder. He had just finished yet another agitated warning when suddenly the cops packed up their apparatus and took it away.

They had bitten off more than they could chew. Expecting a rabble of scared tourists, they found themselves confronting several dozen experienced political activists, not unfamiliar with the inside of police stations. Apprehensive, sure; but we didn't panic and we knew how to fight.

The cops began taking statements from us through an interpreter, but our people refused to sign Indonesian-language transcripts they couldn't read. One frantic officer burst out angrily: "We are the Indonesian police, we are here to help you!" Thank you, constable. Both sides eventually realised what the solution was. I would translate the statements myself. And check the transcripts.

So it is that to this day, somewhere in the files, an American from Melbourne appears on record as interpreter for the Jakarta police.

Eventually the process sped up and we relaxed. This was political and would be resolved higher up; the cops were just going through the motions, and the foreigners could all have got out in a few hours. But one of the Indonesian organisers had been arrested with us. We demanded in vain that they let him leave with us. By this time we'd heard ghastly reports that back at Sawangan, the police had let fanatical religious youth attack the conference organisers with swords. We didn't trust them not to bash this guy if we left him behind.

So most of us spent the night in the Crisis Room, on benches and tiled floors. Staying the night made it seem more dramatic, almost like a state of siege – later in Australia someone would describe it as a "hostage situation". Not quite. We could have gone to hotels. We weren't facing the fearsome treatment Indonesian activists lived with all the time.

And the next evening, Saturday, we did leave, under instructions to come back Monday morning. You should have seen us in the bars that night! The police still held our passports, however, and we figured they'd boot us out of the country. But in next morning's *Jakarta Post* the

Authorities say 29 foreigners free to go

JAKARTA (JP): The Jakarta Police had little to say as immigration Department slammed the police. It seemed the foreigners had used the correct visas after all! It began to look like we'd won the political battle.

Monday morning arrived. We boarded that same shaky bus, and on arrival entered the cop shop. We smiled to police whom we remembered from Friday, but they glared at us. The police force had lost face. Back in the Crisis Room, we endured a pointless tirade from a senior officer we'd never seen before. Then they sent us to the Immigration Department, where we got our passports back. By late afternoon I was in a taxi heading off to a meeting of trade unionists. In a day or two I was on a train out of town. We still wondered why that consulate guy had been so frantic. Then came the announcement: President Wahid, who had cancelled more than one visit to Australia, was finally on his way to Canberra. Maybe they'd been terrified the crazies in the Crisis Room would bring on a diplomatic disaster. What a tempting thought.

WRITING BOOKS

Until 1992, I had been largely concerned with general activism, the daily grind of a small publication, and leading a small group. Having stepped down from the leadership, I turned instead in a direction that allowed me to use my strengths of writing and political analysis, as well as to follow a craving I had had for a long time – writing books.

I had already published a book in 1985. I produced *Into the Mainstream* because the Communist Party of Australia was moving into a Eurocommunist direction and we had something to say about that as revolutionary Marxists. The CPA was growing, and it was convincing people to join it on the basis of a claimed revolutionary ideology. These were people who should have been joining us. We needed to prove that this left turn in the CPA was temporary and superficial, and for that you needed a historical analysis.

In my book I argued that the CPA was no longer Stalinist, but equally that it had not moved towards a revolutionary Marxist perspective. Rather

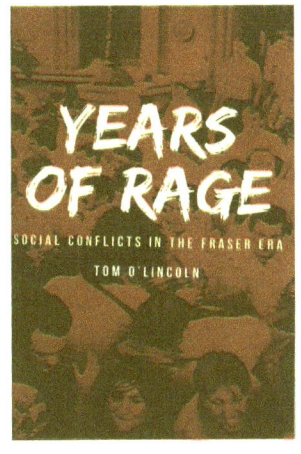

it was moving to assimilate into the political mainstream. By the time the book appeared, this prediction was no longer controversial. The party wound up operations later in the decade.

Into the Mainstream is probably my most successful book and it continues to have a significant following. Socialist Alternative uses it routinely. It shows young readers that there is a history of radical struggle in Australia.

My second book was *Years of Rage. Social Conflicts in the Fraser Era.* Published in 1993, it aimed to capture an experience, in much the same way that Chris Harman caught the '60s and '70s in *The Fire Last Time*. *Years of Rage* covers general strikes, mass anti-nuclear movements, battles against the reactionary Bjelke-Petersen government in Queensland and struggles of the oppressed. I was on the scene of many of the events described. These upheavals, hard fought though they were, generally ended in defeat, which laid the basis for a more quiescent working class under the right wing Labor governments of the '80s and early '90s.

The book was sufficiently successful that we were able to reprint it in 2012. In the Introduction to the revised edition I noted, "The backdrop to this entire complex drama was the global economic crisis of the 1970s and early

1980s. In that regard, the similarities with today will be obvious."

The experience of producing these books gave me a taste for more.

I started writing a book about the history of Australia and had covered the years up to Federation when Phil Griffiths made a convincing argument that the project just didn't hang together. I was in fact writing this book just because I wanted to write a book.

I gave up the larger project, but

the material on pre-Federation Australia was eventually published in 2005 as *United We Stand: Class Struggle in Colonial Australia*. The book contains five essays. The first three cover the history of Australian organised labour from convict times up to Federation. The fourth covers gender and class, with the final essay discussing race and class.

Also coming out of this project was the essay called "'Difficult to get into a black-fellow's head': Black resistance in colonial Australia", which I published online. This essay summarises the work of other historians, most importantly Henry Reynolds, whose books are now the indispensable starting point for any study of Black-white contact and conflict in the Australian colonies. I have no special expertise but I felt the topic was very important, so I provided the text online, and hoped it would serve as an introduction.

The next book was *Class and Class Conflict in Australia* published in 1996, jointly edited by Rick Kuhn and me. We thought there was potential to profile class society, in a compact manner, and produce an accessible book for students that was also affordable. Rick and I wrote a chapter each, with other chapters written by various comrades including Diane Fieldes, Tom Bramble, Mick Armstrong and Janey Stone. The book covers the capitalist class, the working class, labour leaders, migrants, Aborigines, women, racism, and the state. A later enlarged edition, *Class and Struggle in Australia*, edited by Rick Kuhn, was published in 2005.

Rebel Women, co-edited with Sandra Bloodworth and published in 1998, is an anthology of struggles by working class women and women workers in Australia from the late 1800s through the 20th century. It includes accounts from the mining centre of Broken Hill, the Depression, World War II, the post-war years, migrant women in Melbourne, equal pay in the insurance industry and the1986 Victorian nurses' strike. This has been one of the few works that does not treat women as victims, but rather focuses on the way women workers can overcome their oppression and surge into the forefront of activity. Reprinted in 2008, *Rebel Women* continues to be relevant and read today.

My writings were not pioneering in terms of Australian historiography, as they developed themes developed by writers such as Brian Fitzpatrick, Humphrey McQueen, Lynn Beaton and others. My contribution was to give a more rigorous Marxist analysis than these writers.

"Boutique imperialism"

My more recent books have focused on Australian imperialism.

I took up the theme of Australia's role as a colonial settler state, and its role as a minor imperialist power in the region from Humphrey McQueen and developed it further.

The key point is that Australia is imperialist. I developed the concept of "boutique imperialism" to make it easier to grasp how such a small country can be imperialist, by surfing on the back of major imperialist powers. But the Australian imperialist state does not just follow from the larger imperialist states – it demands their backing when it feels threatened.

My book *The Neighbour from Hell* was specifically on this topic. Published in 2014, it was expanded from an essay written for *Class and Class Struggle*, in which I drew together my research on the history of Australian imperialism. Rick Kuhn, in a generous comment in his Introduction to *The Expropriators are Expropriated*, has called this book "a myth-busting historical survey".

Nancy Atkin, who lived next door to me at the time, asked on Facebook whether she was the "neighbour from hell". On the contrary, she is a dynamic community organiser and activist and has been a great friend.

At the book launch, I talked about certain ways the Australian state deploys its troops alongside the great powers like the US, to show how the Australian state fits itself into the structures and dynamics of big-power warfare, without being very big itself.

Here is a slightly edited version of how I described Australia's role in that talk:

> To understand boutique imperialism it might be useful to visualise the Vietnam War. A huge war-making machine trampling everything in its path, and then in the corner somewhere is the Australian contingent, typically a battalion waving the flag. And they do fight, they shoot lots of people, but their main role is to wave the flag and foster the political alliance.
>
> Whenever the government operates this way, it leads to questions from in the public. Why are the Australians in Vietnam when Australia has no obvious material interest in the war? Why is our son overseas getting his head blown off in a place we know nothing about? These questions got some pretty second-rate answers.
>
> From the right wing politicians they got the Pollyanna answers. The war is a noble endeavour. Communism is evil, and so more recently is Islam. We can safely ignore this stuff....
>
> Much more worthy of our respect are the answers they got from the broad Australian left. These are the people who work alongside us in organising committees, and who march alongside us in demonstrations, and they deserve respect. But I don't agree with the answers they traditionally give and which are familiar to us. If Australia is bogged down in Vietnam – or the Gulf, or wherever – it's not because there's any Australian interest in that country. It's because the Americans dragged us in. And if the government in Canberra goes along with this, it's because they're gutless.
>
> This is a psychological theory, not a materialist analysis. I feel like asking: Did Australia have nothing but cowards in the Lodge since Federation? And if so, what's the solution? Assertiveness training? Do we want a more aggressive Tony Abbott? I doubt it. So we end up with the third answer: the Australian bourgeoisie is an imperialist bourgeoisie in its own right. The Australian state is an imperialist state in its own right.

But prior to that book came *Australia's Pacific War*, published in 2011. This work fits with the theme of Australian imperialism, but at the same time, the Pacific War is important for the labour movement in Australia. First because it profoundly affected the lives of millions of workers, but also because the war gave rise to a new kind of nationalism. Where once the left looked on nationalism as, in Ian Turner's words, "the last refuge of the munitions maker", in World War II Communists and other left-of-centre workers and activists embraced what today one can call "left nationalism". Leftists who hate Anzac Day, initially the commemoration of World War 1, are much more open to a patriotism associated with the Kokoda Trail.

Australia's Pacific War brought Marxist categories to the centre of such topics. The arguments I made in that book were vetted by no less an expert than Peter Stanley.

Australia presents its Pacific War effort as a fight for liberation. The book challenged that view. The Allied forces were fighting to re-impose their own imperialist control, and this includes Australia. The Pacific War was best understood as part of a long term pattern of imperialist contention.

The book is sub-titled "challenging a national myth". In using the term "myth" I meant mythology in a more profound sense than usual, somewhat as used by Sorel, to mean a misleading collective ideology.

In an interview, Phil Ferguson asked me what relevance I thought the book had to Australian imperialism – and building opposition to it – today. I replied:

> Not long after the 9/11 attack on the World Trade Center, on the 60th anniversary of Pearl Harbor, US President George [W] Bush made a targeted and insidious speech. On the deck of the USS *Enterprise*, known as a launch pad for American bombing raids in Afghanistan, he told a crowd including 25 witnesses of the battle of Pearl Harbor that the Pacific War had given rise to America's "great calling [which] continues…as the brave men and women of our military fight the forces of terror in Afghanistan and around the world". This sort of thing is the problem I want to fight.[27]

I didn't write the book to convince people not to fight on the Kokoda Trail. I wrote it to show people that the war was not a "noble endeavour" as one historian puts it. This is vital, because the aura of World War II is used to legitimise imperial wars of today.

I.S. IN AUSTRALIA: TAKING STOCK

Writing about your own organisation is full of dangers. You can write a history that shows how the group was always right (except for mistakes triumphantly corrected) or, if you're a hostile ex-member, you can write one about how it was always wrong.

A favourite hybrid is one where the author tells you things went along really well until he or she lost the leadership, and after that it was all downhill. The American socialist Alan Wald remarks: "Surely one of the most tragic features of the history of U.S. Trotskyism is the inability of individuals, who were once comfortable in an organization and then on the 'outs' to recognize problems in theory, practice, and organization until 'one's own ox is gored'."[28] I have tried to avoid these traps.

Have I succeeded? Not entirely. There was one arch-sectarian phase in the 1980s that I sharply opposed, and I still think it was a disgrace, and I've said so. But I have also tried to analyse it as the culmination of a trend in the organisation for which I bear some responsibility myself: the politics of impatience. This is one of two trends that stand out in the history of the International Socialists in Australia. The other is the daring, inspiration and flair that distinguished us at our best from much of the left. It's a fine line.

The group grew dramatically in the 1970s and again in the early 1990s on the basis of its creativity and daring, for example during the 1975 constitutional crisis and the 1991 Gulf War. At other times it did itself serious damage and experienced devastating

Tom with a group of BLF members who were active in the 1986 deregistration struggle at Liz Ross's 60th birthday party in Trades Hall, 2007. Left to right: Tom O'Lincoln, Max Duggan, Jim (Killer) Kane, George Despard, Sal Murru (last BLF Victorian Branch president), Mick Lewis, Margaret Kane

splits, because it tried to force the pace of events. The dramatic struggles of the times were perhaps some excuse for an unrealistic perspective. But we simply didn't have the resources; we were impatient. This was a theme of many political analyses.

When I wrote *Marching Down Marx Street* in 1992, I was aiming at a summary and some clarification of my own ideas of our history and the central issues at dispute up to that point, not a definitive work. I wanted to put our side of the argument, but I also wanted to take into account the ex-leader syndrome – I didn't want to be commenting from the sidelines.

At the end of the essay I responded to a request to sum up "not just the history, but also to summarise what having an IS tradition in Australia has achieved". Here is what I wrote:

> Without us, the demonstrations against Whitlam's sacking or the strikes against Fraser's attacks on Medibank would never have taken on such a radical edge. We have helped create a socialist tradition that looks specifically to the rank and file in the unions and in campaigns, and seeks to challenge conservative bureaucracies.

Tom O'Lincoln speaking from the floor at a packed out session on the British SWP's industrial strategy in the 1970s at Socialist Alternative's union activism and history conference, 17 October, 2015. Photo: James Plested

These contributions to real struggles are complemented by the creation of an intellectual tradition committed to socialism-from-below…

Most importantly, our type of politics now has an organised presence around Australia. Groups associated with the International Socialist current represent a significant portion of the far left.

We have contributed much, and we can contribute much more if we get our act together.

The issue of impatience remains relevant and, given the relatively modest aims of the *Marching Down Marx Street*, it is interesting that I come across people even today who find something useful in reading it. While the fault lines of the 1995 split seemed very different to those of a decade earlier, I would argue that the root explanation was the same: impatience.

And I find the comment that Tony Cliff made at a talk at the Marxism Conference in London in 1984 still very apt:

> It takes nine months to get a baby. That's a fact of life. If you try to get it after two months, you don't get a baby, you get a miscarriage… The number of miscarriages in the revolutionary movement is astonishing. And you know why? Because they always look to the final aim, they don't look to the reality where they are. And therefore they bluff, and they cheat, and the only people they cheat is themselves… I keep saying to comrades: "Be relaxed, be relaxed; don't worry; don't exaggerate"… And that's why when people tell me there is a faction fight in the organisation, there is tension in the organisation, there is nastiness, poisonous nastiness, I tell you straight, it terrifies me galore. It means they don't know the truth about themselves.

A LIFE WORTH LIVING

I have been a Marxist for half a century. In that time I have participated in and been witness to great struggles and momentous historical events. I've had the privilege of standing shoulder to shoulder with selfless fighters around the world. Those events and the people involved only confirmed in my mind that human liberation can be won through the mass struggles of the working class.

Yet sometimes our greatest tests relate to how we deal with extended periods of relative calm. I have returned again and again to the question of impatience. On one hand, all of us need a healthy dose of it – we need to grasp the moment and do what we can, with whatever resources we have, to make the most of any opportunity. On the other hand, there is always a temptation to bridge by force of will the gap between the meagre forces of the revolutionary left and the ultimate end we desire. I have spent my life building small groups, whose primary tasks have been political clarification and recruitment measured in the ones, twos and tens, rather than the hundreds and thousands. That was the only thing circumstances allowed. I watched, again and again, attempts to push beyond what is possible. These always fail.

Of course, there is always cause to say: "If we were bigger we could do this or that". We are constantly aware of the opportunities that go begging because the left is so weak and the group is so small. But attempts to force the pace invariably leave us more isolated rather than in a position of greater influence. Many dedicated people have

Tom at an Rail Train and Bus Union protest 4 September 2015. Photo: Viktoria Ivanova

been left isolated because their group pushed beyond the possible and either destroyed itself or burned out its best activists in the process. Some groups made the opposite mistake and isolated themselves by focusing too much on mechanical party building, and missed opportunities to relate to the wider world. Socialist Alternative, for whatever errors we have made, has navigated between these dangers better than most.

The partisan nature of politics will usually guarantee that we pay an unfair price for our imperfections and our errors. But revolutionaries have to be honest, acknowledging our mistakes and our successes equally. The greatest damage done to us – and I mean the revolutionary left as a whole in the West, where we operate legally and without much state harassment – is often self-inflicted. Half a century since I joined the International Socialists, we are still small. Certainly the political tide has been against us, but we are also weaker for the moments we have let pass.

Why be a revolutionary socialist today? It's a life worth living. There are a lot of frustrations. There are a lot of failures. There are many hours spent performing thankless tasks. Being a revolutionary socialist is difficult. But it is also rewarding. We are at our best and our most human when we prove that we won't give up in the face of a seemingly undefeatable inhuman capitalist system. You can fight without being a socialist, of course. But, as Marx insisted, the purpose of theory is to understand society in order to change it. The method of analysis that he developed, and which continues to be built on by other revolutionaries, is the key to understanding capitalism. In the 21st century, people can find it curious that people like me continue to read Marx, to write about Marx and to teach younger comrades about Marx. Well, it's because he was right.

The working class in the West today may be atomised, showing few signs of the power it displayed in my formative years of the 1960s and early 1970s. But it won't remain so. On a world scale it is much bigger than in Marx's day, and the major contradictions of the capitalist system remain – socialised production for private appropriation and the tendency to crisis. When the workers' movement rises again, the potential for advance will become obvious. Every mass movement associated with the working class has, in whatever confused way, identified with and been a call for human liberation.

Why join an organisation, rather than simply be part of the broader struggle as an individual? Because organisation is necessary for bringing clarity to a situation, and clarity is essential for the actions we take. To have clarity, political debate is required – not for its own sake, but so that we have disciplined and coordinated action based on a realistic assessment of what it possible. Recognising what is possible is a collective effort.

No organisation is perfect. All organisations make mistakes. We commit ourselves, we fight it out and we learn. When we get it right, we advance. When we get it wrong, we try to correct. We do these things under the penalty of being judged not to have lived. I think of the poem by Bertolt Brecht "To those born later":

> *When you speak of our failings*
> *Bring to mind also the dark times*
> *That you have escaped….*
>
> *But you, when the time comes at last*
> *When man is helper to man*
> *Think of us*
> *With forbearance.*[29]

THE HIGHWAY IS FOR GAMBLERS

The highway is for gamblers, better use your sense
Take what you have gathered from coincidence
The empty handed painter from your streets
Is drawing crazy patterns on your sheets
This sky, too, is folding under you
And it's all over now, Baby Blue.
[…]
Leave your stepping stones behind, something calls for you
Forget the dead you've left, they will not follow you
The vagabond who's rapping at your door
Is standing in the clothes that you once wore
Strike another match, go start a new
And it's all over now, Baby Blue.

Bob Dylan, "It's all over now, Baby Blue"

My own journey started in the US and Europe, moved on to distant Australia and encompassed many other parts of the world. A political journey is always a collective experience. Many people have accompanied me in my journey along the highway of revolutionary socialism. I would like to mention some here.

Although no individual stands out, the time I spent as a member of the German SDS was a seminal time in my life, and I learned a great deal from my comrades there.

My time in the Berkeley IS gave me invaluable grounding that guided me for the rest of my journey. Joel Geier was a major mentor and it was a pleasure to meet him again at Marxism 2016 and record our reminiscences about those days. Many other Americans influenced me when I lived there and afterwards. In no particular order they include Kay Eisenhower, Hal Draper, Joel Jordan and Mike Parker.

My story is also partly the history of the organisations of which I was a member, most importantly a small revolutionary current in Australia.

In terms of Australian comrades who have accompanied me on my journey, I think Rick Kuhn is the outstanding figure. There is nobody like him for being able to combine principle and ideas. Rick is a thinker about the nature of Australian capitalism and to me he stands out on this question. Rick could also stand out at times by being difficult and challenging – he wasn't afraid of being controversial.

Rick is in some ways a theoretical coach for the group. My collaborations with Rick are mainly to do with the dynamics of capitalism in Australia, but also in the international context. That has required thinking about the world system as a whole and where it is going. It has been so rewarding to work with him. You'd ring him, and hear the familiar voice, and you'd think, "we're safe". He is a generous collaborator and a delight to work with.

During the Movement Against Uranium Mining in Queensland in the 1980s, Sandra Bloodworth emerged as the best street agitator I had ever seen. Ironically the arrival of the downturn meant she had to rapidly develop in another direction – as a talented propagandist. This has taken an enduring form through the *Marxist Left Review* which publishes material way beyond what Socialist Alternative's (SAlt) small numbers would lead one to expect. Among these are her own original interpretations of Lenin.

Some of the people from Melbourne who figure in and helped produce this book, March 2017. Left to right: Ben Hillier, Robert Zocchi, Viktoria Ivanova, Tom O'Lincoln (centre), Liz Ross, Sandra Bloodworth, Fleur Taylor, Janey Stone

Mick Armstrong, the larrikin of 1974, soon became an organisation builder. My perception of Mick's recent success is that he responds to major problems by calling for debate. This is essentially what our faction called for in 1984-85. It was at the core of Socialist Alternative's sophisticated handling of the fusion with the Revolutionary Socialist Party in 2013. It is doubtful whether anyone else could have handled this process with such a deft hand. The result at one blow established SAlt's position as the leading left group in Australia.

Diane Fieldes has accomplished an astonishing marathon as a leader, holding Sydney branch together for years with total dedication. She must take a huge amount of credit for the breakthrough in that branch, which has developed and grown enough to be running the highly successful Socialism conferences. SAlt is now bigger than any other group on the left there. Diane has also written profiles of the Australian working class with an authority few could match.

Unfortunately I don't know Diane as well as I would like to as we live in different cities. But we do get together periodically for what we jokingly call "old people's discussion".

Tom Bramble is another marathon runner. Although isolated within a small local branch in Brisbane, he found ways to establish himself as a national leader. At the same time he built a strong branch and emerged as an expert on Marxist economics while sustaining an impressive academic career.

Without being simplistic, one could see Mick, Sandra, Tom and Diane as the driving force in the leadership that built SAlt as we know it today.

Many other people have travelled with me on the highway.

Tess Lee Ack was there right at the start on day one in 1972, and is still there today. At a certain point, she made a decision, as I did, that she didn't want to be at the top leadership level. She was perfectly qualified to be there all the time if she had wanted. But in the end, the role she chose for herself was an intelligent choice. She is a person you can always count on and she has made a great contribution.

David Lockwood was a dissident among the cadre. A long time successful local organiser in Melbourne, he spent the latter stages of his work in the group locked into conflicts with some other members of the leadership. A charming man, David distinguished himself as a talented orator able to draw tears and laughter

in equal measure.

I have also enjoyed the comradeship and friendship of many other people at one time or another, some members of my organisation, others outside. The contributions of Alec Kahn, Dave Nadel, Phil Griffiths and Jeff Goldhar have been acknowledged earlier. Others include Ian Rintoul, Darren Rosso, Nancy Atkin, Phil Ferguson, Fleur Taylor, Judy McVey, David Glanz, Graham Willett, Leon Zembekis, Georgia Green, Dave Kerin and Max Lane. In Indonesia they include Budi, Zaki, Surya, Luki, Margianto, Mahendra and Adi.

Last but not least come three people.

Liz Ross is above all a fighter. I first saw her at a demonstration against anti-abortion bigots and was impressed. "That's Liz," said the people around me, "She gives them heaps." Liz's books are a very different side of her, but they are far from academic. They capture struggles from the building industry to the gay rights movement.

Janey Stone is my oldest friend and the hero of this book project. A pioneer of women's liberation and the International Socialism tendency in Australia, she has reinvented herself as a left wing publisher.

Although most of this book is about my life up to the 1990s, I kept travelling into the 21st century. A year into retirement I was diagnosed with Parkinson's Disease. At first this did not stop me from roaming the world. With Jane Tovey, an environmentalist, I visited Bolivia and the Amazon and explored Sumatran rainforests, which gave me a new appreciation of the immediacy of the global environmental crisis. To Jane I owe special thanks for supporting me in many ways, including during a life-threatening health crisis. Without her care and attention this book could not have been written.

Tom with Jane Tovey
in the Sumatran jungle
2004

Endnotes

1. **Page 16** Wernher von Braun, previously a Nazi who invented the V-2 rocket, moved to the US where he worked on intermediate range ballistic missiles and subsequently led the US space program in the 1950s and 60s. Some readers might remember the Tom Lehrer song about him: "Don't say that he's hypocritical/Say rather that he's apolitical/'Once the rockets are up, who cares where they come down?/That's not my department,' says Wernher von Braun".

2. **Page 21** "Herbert's foster parents in America were well meaning, but not having had children of their own were oblivious to the bullying by their older orphan nephews of this defenceless little boy so far from home." Adina Wiens Robinson, *China Beckoning*, Positive Press, Oakland, 1989, p162, footnote.

3. **Page 21** Adina Robinson describes how on Saturday evenings the children had to learn Bible verses in German off by heart, in spite of not knowing the language. They were not allowed to go to bed until they could recite them perfectly. "Herbert had to help us because he knew German. He said to us, 'Now you know why I hate grandpa'."

4. **Page 21** William Cullen Bryant, "Robert of Lincoln", *English Poetry III: From Tennyson to Whitman*, The Harvard Classics 1909-14. Accessed online at http://www.bartleby.com/42/747.html.

5. **Page 23** This story was told in the O'Lincoln family, but does not seem to be known to Tom's cousins. Tom's cousin Charlotte suggests part of the objection to films may have been the immoral lives of Hollywood stars.

6. **Page 33** Delbert Wiens, "From the village to the city", *Direction*, Vol. 2, No. 4, October 1973/January 1974, pp98-149.

7. **Page 34** Hayakawa was to play another role later during a bitter struggle at SF State in 1968-69, when students and the Black Panthers demanded the establishment of an autonomous Black Studies Department. He pulled wires from the loud speakers at a rally.

8. **Page 39** 15 January 1965. Quoted in Hal Draper, *Berkeley, the new student revolt*, chapter 1, https://www.marxists.org/archive/draper/1965/berkeley/ch01.htm.

9. **Page 53** Anonymous correspondent, *Tribune*, 28 June 1968.

10. **Page 72** Barry Sheppard, The Party, Vol. 1: *The Sixties. A Political Memoir*, Resistance Books, Chippendale, 2005.

11. **Page 105** Chris Harman, "The hope of Portugal's revolution", *Socialist Worker* (GB), December 1975.

12. **Page 109** Quoted in Sadie Robinson, "40 years since Portugal's Carnation Revolution", *Socialist Worker* (GB), 22 April 2014.

13. **Page 133** Rick Kuhn, "Class struggle within the state. Thin cats and socialism". *International Socialist*, No 10, August 1980

14. **Page 138** Mick Armstrong, "A million march against 'Camp David'", *The Battler*, 16 February 1980.

15. **Page 144** Slightly edited. Published 20 July 2006 on LEFT-WRITES, blog of Jill Sparrow and Jeff Sparrow (Archived at http://catalogue.nla.gov.au/Record/3791929)

16. **Page 153** Rick Kuhn, "Introduction" in Tom O'Lincoln, *"The expropriators are expropriated" and other writings on Marxism*, Interventions, Melbourne, 2015.

17. **Page 156** Georg Wilhelm Friedrich Hegel, Preface to *The Phenomenology of Mind.*, available at https://www.marxists.org/reference/archive/hegel/phindex.htm.

18. **Page 165** Consejo Superior de la Empresa Privada (Superior Council of Private Enterprise).

19. **Page 170** Jaime Wheelock, "La Nueva Gestión Empresial: Eficiencia, Productividad, Rentabilidad," supplement to *Informaciones Agropecuarias*, División de Communicaciones, MIDINRA, Managua, March-April 1985.

20. **Page 172** Tomás Borge, speech to CDS, *Intercontinental Press*, 24 June 1985.

21. **Page 173** Trabajadores, March 1985.

22. **Page 174** Jaime Wheelock, op.cit.

23. **Page 176** Daniel Ortega, interview, *San Francisco Chronicle*, 6 March 1985.

24. **Page 192** Liz Ross, "Fighting for socialist alternatives", *Socialist Action*, No. 44, October 1989, p4.

25. **Page 196** "Otviety Istorika", *Pravda*, 26 July 1988.

26. **Page 215** Translation by Rufin Kedang

27. **Page 223** "Challenging Australian myths about the war in the Pacific", interview with Philip Ferguson, posted 30 August 2011 at https://rdln.wordpress.com/2011/08/30/demystifying-australian-myths-about-the-war-in-the-pacific/#more-560.

28. **Page 224** George Breitman, Paul Le Blanc and Allan Wald, T*rotskyism in the United States*, Humanities Press, 1996.

29. **Page 229** Bertolt Brecht, "To those born later". Accessed on line at https://macaulay.cuny.edu/eportfolios/smonte10/files/2010/08/Brecht-Born-Later.pdf

Bibliography

Below is a list of material referred to or used as a source in this book. A full list of longer works by Tom O'Lincoln is included in *The expropriators are expropriated,* **Interventions, 2016**

Note: Articles from Tom O'Lincoln's Red Sites will be available at the *Interventions* website www.interventions.org.au

Articles from *Socialist Alternative* magazine can be found online at http://www.sa.org.au/node/3925

Articles from *Red Flag* can be found online at https://redflag.org.au/

Mick Armstrong, "A million march against 'Camp David'", *The Battler*, No. 84, 16 February 1980.

Mick Armstrong, "Another war soon?", *The Battler*, No. 83, 29 March 1980.

Mick Armstrong, *From Little Things Big Things Grow. Strategies for building revolutionary socialist organisations*, Socialist Alternative, Melbourne, 2007. Available online at http://www.sa.org.au/node/4002.

Tomás Borge, speech to CDS, *Intercontinental Press*, 24 June 1985.

George Breitman, Paul Le Blanc and Allan Wald, *Trotskyism in the United States*, Humanities Press, 1996.

Tony Cliff, *Portugal at the Crossroads*. Special issue of *International Socialism* (first series), No. 81/82, September 1975. Available online at https://www.marxists.org/archive/cliff/works/1975/portugal/.

Hal Draper, *Berkeley: The New Student Revolt*, Grove Press, New York, 1965. Available online at https://www.marxists.org/archive/draper/1965/berkeley/ch01.htm.

Abe J. Dueck, "Frank and Agnes Wiens: a remarkable missionary story", *Mennonite Historian*, Vol. 40, No. 1, March 2014, pp2, 4-5. Available online at http://www.mennonitehistorian.ca/40.1.MHMar14.pdf.

Chris Harman, "The hope of Portugal's revolution", *Socialist Worker* (GB), December 1975. Reprinted 11 February 2011 at Socialist Worker.org, https://socialistworker.org/2011/02/11/the-hope-of-portugals-revolution.

Chris Harman, *The Fire Last Time: 1968 and after*, Bookmarks, 2007.

Georg Wilhelm Friedrich Hegel, Preface to *The Phenomenology of Mind.*, available at https://www.marxists.org/reference/archive/hegel/phindex.htm.

Samuel Ichiye Hayakawa, *Language in Thought and Action*, Harcourt Inc., various editions.

Phil Ilton, *The origins of the IS in Australia. A history of the Socialist Workers Action Group*, Melbourne 1978. Published as a pamphlet by the International Socialists in 1984.

Rick Kuhn, "Class struggle within the state. Thin cats and socialism". *International Socialist*, No 10, August 1980

Rick Kuhn, "Introduction" in Tom O'Lincoln, *"The expropriators are expropriated" and other writings on Marxism*, Interventions, Melbourne, 2016

Tom O'Lincoln, "Israel from within", *The Battler*, No. 8, 18 July 1975.

Tom O'Lincoln, "The people behind a thirty years struggle", *The Battler*, No. 83, 29 March 1980.

Tom O'Lincoln, *Into the mainstream: the decline of Australian Communism*, Stained Wattle Press, Westgate (NSW), 1985.

Tom O'Lincoln, "Nicaragua: The Sandinistas, Capitalism and Socialism", *Socialist Action*, Melbourne, 1986.

Tom O'Lincoln, "Gorbachev and the fate of socialism", *Socialist Action* magazine, Melbourne, No. 35, November 1988.

Tom O'Lincoln, *A South American revolutionary: Jose Carlos Mariátegui and Peruvian socialism*, [date?] published online at Red Sites. (A slightly different version of this article appeared in *Socialist Review*, No. 2, Melbourne, Winter, 1990.)

Tom O'Lincoln, *Marching Down Marx Street: The International Socialists in Australia*, 1992. Available online at Red Sites.

Tom O'Lincoln, *Years of Rage: social conflicts in the Fraser era*, Bookmarks Australia, Melbourne, 1993; second edition, Interventions, Melbourne, 2012.

Tom O'Lincoln, "A crisis is also an opportunity. Building revolutionary organisation today", 2002. Available online at Red Sites.

Tom O'Lincoln, "Indonesia: from *reformasi* to reaction", *Socialist Alternative* magazine, No. 80, July 2004.

Tom O'Lincoln, "Nicaragua. The revolution in 1985", revised version August 2004, published online at Red Sites.

Tom O'Lincoln, *United We Stand: Class Struggle in Colonial Australia*, Red Rag, Carlton North, 2005.

Tom O'Lincoln, "'Difficult to get into a black-fellow's head': Black resistance in colonial Australia", n.d. http://www.anu.edu.au/polsci/marx/interventions/kooris.htm.

Tom O'Lincoln, "Child of the space race", October 2006, published online at Red Sites.

Tom O'Lincoln, "What happened to the sixties?", *Socialist Alternative* magazine, No. 128, May 2008.

Tom O'Lincoln, "Nazareth: Dark reports from the holy city", 20 July 2008, published on LEFT-WRITES, blog of Jill Sparrow and Jeff Sparrow (Archived at http://catalogue.nla.gov.au/Record/3791929)

Tom O'Lincoln, "Challenging Australian myths about the war in the Pacific", interview with Philip Ferguson of Redline, posted 30 August 2011 at https://rdln.wordpress.com/2011/08/30/demystifying-australian-myths-about-the-war-in-the-pacific/#more-560.

Tom O'Lincoln, *Australia's Pacific War: challenging a national myth*, Interventions, Melbourne, 2011.

Tom O'Lincoln, "Twenty-five past midnight in Portugal", *Red Flag*, No. 13, 20 November 2013.

Tom O'Lincoln, "A response to Shane Bentley on Portugal", *Red Flag*, No. 17, 13 February 2014.

Tom O'Lincoln, *The neighbour from hell: two centuries of Australian imperialism*, Interventions, Melbourne, 2014.

Tom O'Lincoln, "The real legacy of Malcolm Fraser", *Red Flag*, No. 44, 24 March 2015.

Tom O'Lincoln, "Conspiracy theories about dismissal obscure more important things", *Red Flag*, No. 60, 9 November 2015.

Tom O'Lincoln, "Was it asking for trouble?" (a response to Sean Matgamna, "The Two Trotskyisms confront Stalinism", Workers Liberty, 2015), posted 7 March 2016 at http://www.workersliberty.org/node/26374.

Tom O'Lincoln, "Remembering the 1964 Republican National Convention", *Red Flag*, No. 73, 13 June 2016.

Tom O'Lincoln, *"The expropriators are expropriated" and other writings on Marxism*, Interventions, Melbourne, 2016.

Tom O'Lincoln, edited with Rick Kuhn, *Class and Class Conflict in Australia*, Pearson Longman, Frenchs Forest, 1996.

Tom O'Lincoln, edited with Sandra Bloodworth, *Rebel women in Australian working class history*, Interventions, Melbourne 1998, republished by *Red Rag*, 2007.

Tom O'Lincoln, translated with Setiabudi, *Sosialisme revolusioner: gagasan, strategi dan taktik* (a collection of articles on socialist politics), Kelompok Kerja Bersama, Solo, 2000.

Tom O'Lincoln, with Setiabudi, *Mereka menyebutnya globalisasi*, (translation of Chris Harman, *Anti-capitalism: theory and practice*), Sumbu Press, Yogyakarta, 2002.

Daniel Ortega, interview, San Francisco Chronicle, 6 March 1985.

Adina Wiens Robinson, *China Beckoning*, Positive Press, Oakland, 1989.

Peter Robinson, "Portugal" in Colin Barker (ed.), *Revolutionary Rehearsals*, Haymarket Books, 2002.

Sadie Robinson, "40 years since Portugal's Carnation Revolution", *Socialist Worker* (GB), 22 April 2014. Available online at https://socialistworker.co.uk/art/37973/40+years+since+Portugals+Carnation+Revolution.

Liz Ross, "Fighting for socialist alternatives", *Socialist Action*, No. 44, October 1989, p4.

Liz Ross and Tom O'Lincoln "Shattering the Myth of Exploitation", *Socialist Action* No.45, November 1989, p4.

Liz Ross, *Dare to Struggle, Dare to Win! Builders Labourers fight deregistration, 1981-94*, The Vulgar Press, Carlton North, 2004.

Barry Sheppard, *The Party, Vol. 1: The Sixties. A Political Memoir*, Resistance Books, Chippendale, 2005.

Janey Stone, "Lebanon: the PLO fights on, *The Battler*, No. 83, 29 March 1980.

Janey Stone, "Jeff Goldhar's socialist legacy", *Marxist Interventions* 1, 2009, http://www.anu.edu.au/polsci/mi/1/mi1stone.pdf.

Delbert Wiens, "From the village to the city", *Direction*, Vol. 2, No. 4, October 1973/January 1974, pp98-149. Available online at http://www.directionjournal.org/2/4/from-village-to-city.html.

Frank J. Wiens, *Fifteen years among the Hakkas of South China*, 1930, self-published.

Jaime Wheelock, "La Nueva Gestión Empresial: Eficiencia, Productividad, Rentabilidad," supplement to Informaciones Agropecuarias, División de Communicaciones, MIDINRA, Managua, March-April 1985.

www.ingramcontent.com/pod-product-compliance
Lightning Source LLC
Chambersburg PA
CBHW061153010526
44118CB00027B/2956